PROJECT MANAGEMENT: IT'S ALL BOLLOCKS!

Welcome to *Project Management: It's All Bollocks!* where two people who vaguely know each other and barely like each other will pick over the sadly inadequate body of knowledge that is project management today, and generally challenge just about everything, eliminating that which you don't need to bother to learn about, or should already know, leaving you only with the parts that will give you the results you want. This book is a shakedown of project management, the profession, the myths it creates and promotes, its great ideas and ambitions and a few ropey bits that we're just not convinced about.

The project management profession continues to grow and mature, but is at risk of excluding those who don't fit the mould. There is a mystique out there that only certificated project managers can be project managers. This is nonsense. The project management skill set is accessible to anyone, and how you choose to access it and put it to use should remain the decision of the individual. There shouldn't be a right or wrong choice. This book is targeted at those 'projects as usual project managers' who will drive most of the change inside organisations tomorrow and beyond, and who really need help to do that.

The authors offer up a selection of seven cracking ideas, that when applied to a project environment will ultimately result in you being a good manager of projects in this modern world of business complexity.

SUSIE PALMER-TREW is an award winning project professional and, at the time of going to print, she was Director, Change and Improvement at The Open University, enabling others to get shit done in a world tied up in red tape. She is the co-creator of Open to Change, avid risk taker and professional trouble maker.

PETER TAYLOR is author of the Amazon number 1 bestselling project management book, *The Lazy Project Manager*, and professional speaker, having given 350 lectures around the world in over 25 countries. He has been described as 'perhaps the most entertaining and inspiring speaker in the project management world today'.

PROJECT MANAGEMENT: IT'S ALL BOLLOCKS!

THE COMPLETE EXPOSURE OF THE WORLD OF, AND THE VALUE OF, PROJECT MANAGEMENT

Susie Palmer-Trew and Peter Taylor

Routledge
Taylor & Francis Group

LONDON AND NEW YORK

First published 2020
by Routledge
2 Park Square, Milton Park, Abingdon, Oxon OX14 4RN

and by Routledge
52 Vanderbilt Avenue, New York, NY 10017

*Routledge is an imprint of the Taylor & Francis Group,
an informa business*

British Library Cataloguing-in-Publication Data
A catalogue record for this book is available from the British
Library

Library of Congress Cataloging-in-Publication Data
Names: Palmer-Trew, Susie, 1985- author. | Taylor, Peter,
1957- author.
Title: Project management: it's all bollocks! : the complete
exposure of the world of, and the value of, project
management / Susie Palmer-Trew and Peter Taylor.
Description: Milton Park, Abingdon, Oxon ; New York, NY :
Routledge, 2020. | Includes index.
Identifiers: LCCN 2019041912 (print) | LCCN 2019041913
(ebook) | ISBN 9780367140908 (hardback) |
ISBN 9780429030147 (ebook)
Subjects: LCSH: Project management.
Classification: LCC HD69.P75 P32 2020 (print) | LCC HD69.
P75 (ebook) | DDC 658.4/04–dc23
LC record available at https://lccn.loc.gov/2019041912
LC ebook record available at https://lccn.loc.gov/2019041913

ISBN: 978-0-367-14090-8 (hbk)
ISBN: 978-0-429-03014-7 (ebk)

Typeset in MinionPro
by Integra Software Services Pvt. Ltd.

SUSIE:

To all the rough diamonds, getting by and getting on in a project management world with little room for curiosity.

To Peter.*insert your own compliment here*

And of course, my very own Pigeon and Squab.

PETER:

To Susie for helping me to avoid becoming yet another old fart of the project management world by agreeing to write this book and generally challenging me every step of the way.

And to Juliet; simply, the love of my life.

CONTENTS

THE ACKNOWLEDGEMENTS

SUSIE

M any people have tried to change who I am or who I could be. So, my thanks go to those who didn't try, who accepted, created space and gave me time, to be me.

I love what I do, and I aspire to create momentum, a movement that can do 'it' differently. This is the first step of many.

PETER

I would like to thank everyone who has, in any way, guided and helped me in my career in project management over the past (mumbled large number of) years.

This includes those who have challenged me, my approach, and what I speak about and stand for.

Without such moments, it would be all too easy to assume that you are right; which is not always the case.

THE AUTHORS

SUSIE PALMER-TREW

Susie has worked within project and change environments for the past 10 years, across construction, IT and strategy. Spending most of her time within higher education, she has both an academic and professional interest in project management as an ever-evolving skill, and an emerging culture. Very much at the coal face of project management, she practices what she preaches, always choosing to seek forgiveness, before permission.

With a reputation for delivering impact, and getting results, she balances this through sharing and spreading the passion she has for her work, to enable team-mates, peers and leaders to deliver successful organisation-wide change.

At the point of going to print, she was Director, Change and Improvement at The Open University, enabling a complex, unique and treasured institution to keep its traditions alive by enabling its fires to burn bright into the future.

- Generally known for being wonderfully sarcastic and not giving a fuck (and for being very competent and ever the professional).

PETER TAYLOR

Peter Taylor is a PMO/Project/Change expert who has built and led five global PMOs across several industries and has advised many other organisations in change and transformation strategy. He is also the author of the Amazon number 1 bestselling project management book, *The Lazy Project Manager*,[1] along with many other books on project leadership, project marketing, project challenges and executive sponsorship, three of which are published by Gower Publishing: *Leading Successful PMOs*,[2] *Delivering Successful PMOs*[3] and *The Social Project Manager*.[4]

Peter has delivered over 350 lectures around the world in over 25 countries, and has been described as 'perhaps the most entertaining and inspiring speaker in the project management world today'.

- Generally known as being 'lazy' and writing short (but hopefully useful and entertaining) books.[5]

1 *The Lazy Project Manager: How to be Twice as Productive and Still Leave the Office Early* (Infinite Ideas Limited, 1st edn, 2009; 2nd edn, 2015).
2 *Leading Successful PMOs: How to Build the Best Project Management Office for your Business* (Gower Publishing, 2011).
3 *Delivering Successful PMOs: How to Design and Deliver the Best Project Management Office for your Business* (Gower Publishing, 2015).
4 *The Social Project Manager: Balancing Collaboration with Centralised Control in a Project Driven World* (Gower Publishing, 2015).
5 Susie: Also known for being really fucking modest.

THE NON-FOREWORD

Normally, in a book of this nature, you would find here a short commentary by some learned and influential person (typically someone who will help the authors and their publishers 'sell' the book to a wider audience, whilst also helping the authors by putting a stamp of approval on their work) but in reality, in the context of this book, that would be someone talking bollocks about bollocks wouldn't it?

And so, as a result of an attempt at integrity by the authors, this section is left blank(ish) intentionally.

Here is a picture of Susie and Peter having an Espresso Martini, to make up for brevity.

The authors enjoying an Espresso Martini whilst not talking bollocks

THE INTRODUCTION

This book is a 'shakedown'. Bold opening statement!

It's a shakedown of project management, the profession, the myths it creates and promotes, its great ideas and ambitions and a few ropey bits that we're just not too damn convinced about.

Of course, this shakedown is completely subjective. It is written by two very independent minds, with little, but some, consultation, but written from a perspective of valuing our profession and acknowledging what it has achieved over the years.

Let's start this old shakedown by meeting the minds behind the book.

SUSIE

So why write a book to tell someone or something they are wrong, when it could probably be done in a slightly awkward email?

Because that's not what we are doing. We're debating a few hot topics that we feel are recurring within the industry, or just never answered to any degree of acceptability. This is balanced by challenging you, the reader, to look up from your respective parapet, out of the box, over the wall, from behind the hedge, etc. and start taking notice. It is not about proving that something is 'wrong'.

Project management has evolved, and we believe it will continue to do so through the great work of the professional communities and the professional bodies who support its development, and the people who reside within it. The industry will continue to grow as the world continues to change, the lines between project management and change management will blur and clarify as much as they converge and diverge. Projects will both succeed and fail, the sector will continue to talk of lessons learnt, most of us will still love dashboards, our executives will still be scared of 'Red' status reports and the majority of us will probably do as we've always done and mistakes will repeat, repeatedly. We'll stop talking about 'digital' and 'transformation' as it will either be a phase, or it will no longer be fancy enough to talk about. We'll probably have made our peace with Agile (methodology) and agile (the attitude). But we will still be using a core skill set to deliver new things, delivering value to people and processes, we'll still be building and changing things. We'll still be project managers and we'll probably think something else is just bollocks.

We aim to challenge ourselves, through the writing of this book and those who choose to read it, to push some boundaries, challenging the status quo in order to 'do differently'. Opening doors to the new, the different, the open-minded and the 'not quite sure', together with those of us who feel at risk of being stifled and misdirected through the attitude and expectations of the mature project management community (and by 'mature' we clearly mean 'stuck in their ways').

Whilst I feel that writing this so early on may disappoint some, there is no intent to undermine or undo the work of professional bodies and organisations that have fought to have project management recognised as a profession, that bring best practice to the forefront and support millions fulfilling project management roles in tackling complex, volatile and sometimes bonkers problems. It is written to create not destroy.

We want to create space. Space is a skill set that has catapulted itself into a profession built on bodies of knowledge, traditional sectors and singular ways of thinking. The project management profession continues to grow and mature (and that's great) but is at risk of excluding those who don't quite fit the mould (and that's not so great).

This book is for 'business as usual' project managers, 'square peg, round hole' project managers, the 'sorry, I'm not a project manager' project managers and the 'actually yes, it is a proper job' project managers, those who will drive most of the change inside organisations tomorrow and beyond, and who really need help to do that.

This book is for people like me, who every so often need to check-in with themselves, their ambition and their attitude.

We're trying to write the book I wish someone else had written, so that I could read it. The book I would have reached for when, at the tender age of 21 and working on some of my first projects, I told my manager to Fuck Off because I thought I knew better (evidence suggested otherwise). It would have been the book whose pages I would have flicked through as I battled with poor career choices looking for inspiration and a bit of help, and probably the book I wish I had thrown across the room at the person who told me I wouldn't succeed. It would have been the book I would eventually use to wedge a door open (before I got a trophy to do that job for me).

PETER

As someone who has been in this 'profession' (scary word to use with regard to project management it seems for some, but you have to call it something) for an awful lot of years, I realised that my revolutionary and challenging days may be coming to an end. There is a new generation driving their way into my world and I welcome them and wish them well in my 'profession', I'm sure that they can do a far better job that I have.

When I wrote *The Lazy Project Manager* back in 2009 it was different, it was unusual, perhaps even radical in some ways, and it was all about managing yourself whilst managing projects, plus it was written with love and heavy doses of fun and honesty. Critically, it was written with complete freedom (thank you publishers for knowing nothing at all about project management at that time).

Since then, I have been part of, and been an observer of, the explosive growth in change, in projects and therefore in project management, much of which I love but some of which I don't like quite so much.

Therefore perhaps, with the aid of my co-author, this might well be my farewell contribution to project management. One last irreverent but earnest offering up to the many, many 'project' involved people around the world. Something that can really help them in their change delivering, business transforming work, however big or however small, and something that will make them stop and think.

In my view there are three components of organisational activity these days: business as usual (of course), projects as projects (pure and simple/complex), but also what I refer to as 'projects as usual' (change, managed as part of the daily work of business people who may or may not have 'project manager' in their title or even resume).

As Susie has well stated, we aim this book at the new, the different, the open-minded, and the 'not quite sure'. As a true 'accidental' project manager all those years ago, I really could have done with something in those early days, in fact anything that was readable, practical, real and simple to reference. I'm not sure I was even a 'rough diamond' at that time, but I somehow survived in the project world (long before I realised I was actually in the project world) and can only thank all of those I have learned from over time, and those who tolerated my mistakes.

Change delivery is a wonderful world that needs to be inclusive, open, sharing and free of all that stuff that is clearly 'bollocks'.

Bold closing statement! But we hope that you are hooked and will read on. Shame not to, really.

THE BOOK

The book has three major chapters.

Chapter 1 looks at some of the things that really annoy the fuck out of us with regard to the profession we both live and breathe. Just some stuff that is wholly 'bollocks' in most cases and which we all need to put into the great big dumpster of working life and move on, big time.

Chapter 2 is the really useful chapter (at least we think it is). The chapter where we filter out all the crap, distill the good down to the bare minimum, and present the seven key principles of being an effective project manager in the modern world.

And lastly, Chapter 3 is where we offer some thoughts (and guidance) on the world in which you will attempt to be that effective project manager – the critical five influences on your personal success chart.

Of course, there is a chapter where all of this succinct thought summarisation is, in fact, even further reduced to the essential elements of getting shit done (Chapter 4). We have tried to make this really easy for you.

And how can you not love a book that includes advice such as 'Start running into rooms and shouting "SURPRISE". People won't like it, but it might mean they think twice before they do it to you'.

Awesome!

Never mind the bollocks. Do not let others define you. Keep working for what you believe in. Do not give up.

Richard Branson

CHAPTER ONE

The bloody annoying world of project management

Here the authors will discuss and challenge some of the assumptions, presumptions and generally weird stuff that they see and hear around project management. And trust us, there is a whole lot of said assumptions and presumptions going around and around the project world, and the amount of weird stuff can easily leave you gob-smacked at times.

THE PREMISE

First, let's get a very important definition out of the way:

Definition: 'Bollocks' nonsense; rubbish (used to express contempt or disagreement, or as an exclamation of annoyance).[1]

---

1 'Bollocks' is a word of Middle English origin, meaning 'testicles'. The word is often used figuratively in colloquial British English as a noun to mean 'nonsense', an expletive following a minor accident or misfortune, or an adjective to mean 'poor quality', 'useless' or 'unnecessary'.

Is that clear? Good. If not, then you can read a longer definition in the footnote below.

Definition over then we can proceed to the asking of the all-important question.

Is it 'Bollocks' or 'Not Bollocks', that is, indeed, a question; a question William Shakespeare never asked for sure, or if he did he never put it in writing as far as we know, but it is a question we are asking in his place.

To be fair, the is it 'Bollocks' or 'Not Bollocks' is probably not 'The' number one question of life, the universe and everything, but nevertheless it is a question that we feel needs asking and one that we, the authors, are not afraid to ask (many times over, in fact).

But we are also here to provide some answers, as best we can, after all, what is the point of a book that poses only questions without any possible responses? In doing this, we believe that we are both balanced and informative, or at least we try to be.

If you break down the whole 'Is it bollocks?' biggy question into smaller bite size consumable points of interest, then we find ourselves (well the authors do anyway) considering such weighty matters as 'What the hell is project management?' and 'What is my project

---

Americans will freely use the word 'bullshit' in the place of 'bollocks', but the authors much prefer the Anglo-Saxon as a less offensive or aggressive word, and it only works as a negative.

Whilst common phrases such as 'Bollocks to this!' and 'That's a load of old bollocks' generally indicate contempt for a certain task, subject or opinion (negative), conversely, the word also figures in idiomatic phrases such as 'the dog's bollocks' or more simply 'the bollocks' (as opposed to just 'bollocks'), which will refer to something which is admired, approved of or well-respected (positive).

Yes, it is confusing, but that's life, and 'bollocks' is a damn useful word, we hope that you will agree.

identity?', along with a hint of 'Do I need to be certified?' thrown in for good measure. We get asked that a lot!

These questions allow us to drift seamlessly into other critical queries, such as 'Who owns project management?' and 'Do all projects need a project manager?', before exploring that wonderful old chestnut of 'Why are there so many twats in project management?'; no doubt, all things that you have asked yourself on a regular basis.

And let's not leave it there; we have more to cover, and so let's drive straight into a big finish with 'Why is nobody ever to blame?' – a perfect conclusion to this complete 'bollocky' assessment, the purpose of which is to de-clutter the conversations that follow in Chapter 2 'Seven cracking ideas' and Chapter 3 'The art of getting shit done and staying cool', which are the real 'meaty' chapters (unless you are pescatarian, vegetarian or vegan, in which case please insert the equivalent word from your personal belief world).

Whatever your life choice with regard to food might be, we should all be bollocks intolerant.

OK, let's go.

WHAT THE HELL IS PROJECT MANAGEMENT, ANYWAY?

"Here's one to mess with your emotions straight away, what actually is project management?" enquired Susie.

"It's the management of projects", replied Peter, confident in his response.

facepalm

"It's going to be a long old day", retorted Susie with barely concealed contempt.

"What?" panicked Peter, "It is, isn't it?".

"Well, you are technically accurate whilst skilfully being completely bloody wrong", answered Susie, "Well done, it must be a gift!".

"Harsh", sulked Peter.

"Let's talk".

B eginning simply is often the best way.

So, you are reading a book about project management, therefore surely you know what we're on about?

That might be true, and this may feel all a bit primitive as a result, but with so many definitions, so many expectations and way too many assumptions out there, we thought it sensible (for once) to start with the obvious.

As we said, beginning simply is often the best way.

The world, workplace and expectations are very different now from when most project managers got their feet under the table (insert age statistic here). So, it's only fair to suggest that what we include in or consider part of a definition around project management must also be different.

The idea that project management is just the management of things to deliver specific goals and meet specific success criteria at the specified time are drifting off into the sunset (and thank the good lord for that, we say). The days of being 'exact' are becoming few and far between, as are the days of delivering projects in 'controlled environments'. Project management is transitioning more to it being the art of 'getting weird stuff done', usually to improve a situation or to realise an opportunity.

The need for a project usually arises to solve the problems that shouldn't be there in the first place (risk and issue management) or to achieve strategic gain (opportunity and advantage). How we respond to these two scenarios will always depend on what's 'under the hood'.

There are many methodologies and associated processes on project management, which have all served a purpose and really helped project teams deliver big changes, but these models and definitions have been developed largely to deal with stable, controlled and understood environments, where the expectation is detailed through firm requirements and deliverables.

Now we're not throwing the baby out with the bath water, and this book isn't a new model or hot exciting method, but we believe that the current offer is a bit bollocks and will never fully meet the need of project teams as we transition into project delivery within ever-changing, ambiguous, complex and uncertain environments and ideals, especially in a socially connected and collaborative business world.

We feel that the need to redefine or to simply be open to new definitions around project management is crucial for your career and your sanity, if nothing else. The same redefinition or openness is required in order to address the changes to success measurement that exist in this 'new world' (a few moments of quiet reflection for the 'good old days' of the triple constraint or iron triangle can be understandable at this difficult time for some readers – OK, that's it, reminiscence over, move on).

We believe that a project must be any combination (but not necessarily all) of the following:

- Unique
- Messy
- Ambiguous
- Complicated (or complex)
- Unpredictable
- Uncertain
- Needed (through choice, or regulation)
- Scalable (not necessarily repeatable)
- Disruptive (in a good way)
- Risky (again, in a good way)
- Make 'things' 'better'
- And, generally, not 'business as usual'

And the management of said activity should be within agreed tolerances determined by you and your environment, all wonderfully enabled through open dialogue and honesty (both inward and outward).

So, what does project management boil down to?

We reckon it is the temporary provision of structure and transparency in order to solve short-term, complicated problems or to realise opportunities.

Sometimes it is really bloody hard and sometimes it is just bloody fantastic.

But is it bollocks?

Of course ... not – we've written an entire book on it!

But most importantly as project managers, we need to be able to articulate the change we're delivering, why we're doing it and how we're going to land it; and that, my friends, is where we start to blur the lines between project management (the process of delivery) and change management (the understanding and acceptance of delivery).

The above asks and answers the question 'What is project management?'. In *The Lazy Project Manager*, the author talks of a very typical situation in the project management world where you might ask project managers what they are. It goes like this and is something to play at project management parties. You ask two questions of a project manager and they have to respond with the first thing that comes into their head. Most of the time it goes down like this: 'What are you?' – 'I'm a project manager'; 'What do you do?' – 'I manage projects'. Insightful, isn't it?

NOBODY PUTS BABY IN THE CORNER (WHAT IS MY IDENTITY?)

"Who are ya? Who are ya?" Peter bellowed in his best 'lads at the football match voice'.

"FFS", Susie said, "you know who I am, what are you on about now?"

"How do people know who you are and what you do, when even you can't explain it?" Peter questioned.

"Who says I can't?" Susie cut him off.

"OK, go on then", Peter responded in a slightly fractious tone.

Awkward silence.

"Fair enough", Susie continued, "your question, I believe, is really: 'How do you build and identify as a project manager when there is the perception that we should be "seen and not heard"?'"

"Exactly", nodded Peter, "although I doubt there's anyone who doesn't hear you coming".

Susie glared.

"I said that out loud didn't I?" Peter queried nervously.

Susie's expression answered the question without the need for anything to be said.

"Let's talk …".

I f you are in project management, you know that that this is a fun job.

OK, yes, there are days that it is incredibly hard, it is usually messy and complicated, and nine times out of ten, as a project manager, you can't do right for doing wrong. But it's great to be able to use our skill set to deliver value in an ever-changing world, to those needing it. In fact, it is more than great if we are all honest here, it is pretty ace all round.

However, outside your project world, others will most likely acknowledge that it is a job, a role that is growing in both the opportunity and number of people in it but, probably, no one has ever been to a party and said, 'I'm a project manager' and anybody's got really excited about it; it's no great conversation starter.

And it doesn't let up in the work environment with the often-said instant response of 'oh here come the fun police!', which is always amazingly motivational (not). Project managers are perceived as the people who stop others from doing things, they control how they do it, and – adding insult to injury – they slow things down. Worse than that, the growing idea that project managers (and everyone else tasked with leading significant change) are there to obfuscate, to hide the truth and to 'trick' those affected by a project to 'get on with it and ask questions later'. People (read non-project folk) have developed caricatures of project managers of both the inept (Dilbert[2]) and the calculated (Fyre Festival[3]). And of course, there's the 'witty brigade' who call us project manglers.

So how do you form a professional identity when it feels like those around you are doing it on your behalf? When the 'brand' of your profession already feels like it's in a losing battle. We reckon a professional identity involves a mix of knowledge, credibility and expertise and, of course, your own personality, and it is these identities that create a distinction among the people in our profession who have similar backgrounds, and create utter confusion to those outside it. How do we harness our best bits, to showcase our individual identity without throwing those around us under a bus?

Let's go back to the beginning, when we talk about 'project managers', many people think we don't do anything useful and those who know what we do distil it down to two key components: (1) we boss people around and (2) we make sure nobody wins.

---

2 Dilbert is an American comic strip written and illustrated by Scott Adams.
3 Fyre Festival was a failed luxury music festival founded by Billy McFarland, CEO of Fyre Media Inc, and rapper Ja Rule. During the Fyre Festival's inaugural weekend, the event experienced problems related to security, food, accommodation, medical services and artist relations, resulting in the festival being postponed indefinitely.

The trouble is, they're not that far off.

As a project manager, you are piggy in the middle, arbitrating between competing sides who ultimately will want different things during the project lifecycle. There will always be different teams (stakeholders, departments, etc.) fighting for different goals and wanting to achieve different outcomes or priorities. As a project manager, your job is to make sure that nobody wins. You are the one who has to always think of the whole, not letting anyone 'improve' their own outcomes at the expense of another.

We're not often popular, we take the blame, often, even when it's not ours to take and sometimes we're not aware that we're being blamed. We always have someone else's best interest at heart; when you're with your team, you represent your sponsor or client; when you're with your sponsor, you represent your team. Our success is not measured in what we achieve, it's measured by what those around us accomplish and what the project delivers. It's not about you, it's about everyone else.

And it's that very premise that can make it hard to form an 'identity' as a project manager, one that you recognise and that is accessible to the world beyond project management. Arguably, there are ways to be identified, if your projects are tangible (construction, engineers, political) or branded (Brexit,[4] Olympics), or if you have been recognised by your peers or professional bodies (shout out to all those award winners). But this is all temporary (and maybe rightly so), you only sing when you're winning, and when that moment passes, or becomes too distant, then your identifier leaves the room on the back of your trophy.

---

4 Brexit is the withdrawal of the United Kingdom (UK) from the European Union (EU). Following a referendum held in 2016 in which 51.9% of those voting supported leaving the EU, the Government invoked Article 50 of the Treaty on European Union, starting a supposed two-year process.

So, the next time someone asks you what you do, don't leave them thinking it's all bollocks.

If you play the project manager party game of two questions, answer them fast, with the first thing that comes to mind. As we said earlier, the usual scenario of: 'What are you?', answer 'A project manager'; 'What do you do?', answer 'I manage projects' results in confusion and general bewilderment, along with the likelihood of not being invited to any of the cool parties in the future.

Instead, tell them about enabling others to succeed, about needing to know everything without trying, that tackling adversity and controversy is just part of your day job, share a story of the impact you made, or the footprint you left behind and do it with the passion and control that you harness in your 'day job'. Find ways to bring your expertise to light, to share it outside your professional circles or activities. Showcase what you can do and be really bloody proud of it.

Lead with your stories, of your successes, and leave your job title in the office (because that probably is a load of bollocks as well).

WHO OWNS PROJECT MANAGEMENT?

"I am Spartacus[5]", announced Susie.

"What are you on about now?" asked Peter in an exasperated tone.

---

5 The phrase refers to a scene in the movie 'Spartacus' starring Kirk Douglas. After the army of former Roman slaves led by Spartacus is defeated in battle by the Roman army, a Roman general stands before the captured surviving members of the slave army and demands that they turn over Spartacus, or else all of the former slaves will be executed. Upon hearing this and not wanting his friends to be executed, Spartacus stands up and says, 'I am Spartacus'. However, the loyalty of his friends is so great that each of them stands forward in succession, shouting 'I am Spartacus!' until the shouts dissolve into a cacophony of thousands of former slaves each insisting 'I am Spartacus!'.

"I am project management is what I mean", explained Susie.

"Well I am project management then", Peter responded.

"Exactly my point", smiled Susie, "we are all project management and therefore we, collectively, own project management and not some corporate style self-defined and self-imposed organisation or anyone else for that matter".

"Totally agree", Peter said in a totally agreeable manner.

"Nice to hear that for a change", Susie said, "infinite monkeys and all that, bound to happen eventually", she laughed.

"You're most welcome", smiled Peter, confused but putting a brave face on it anyway.

"Let's talk …".

As humans we have an 'inherent' desire to belong and to feel that we are an important part of something greater than ourselves, in the case of project management we want to (and often choose to be part of a global project community, but in doing so we have created the need that someone should 'own it', be the custodian, provide control and guidance, therefore creating an opportunity to be 'owned'. And here come the professional bodies, marching over the horizon, just in time to give us all a safe haven (or haven of choice).

This is not limited to our project world; it is partly just human nature.

Pretty much everything in life, whether it be politics, unions, corporations, etc., evolves to a point where the active minority, by default of their activity, become the owners, typically by default of their relative inactivity. This is because the rest of the people want the relationship, the closeness to the community, but don't want to take responsibility for curating or creating it, they have other matters to take care of in life.

And the result of this need to be owned, and the desire for a 'home' is the development of competing approaches and methods, and standards and language, and mantras, and all manner of dark arts forging groups and relationships that can fulfil the human need for control as well as also the professional need for control to ensure safety, consistency and equal competition.

Consider a profession such as architecture, there's only one way of doing it. Aesthetics aside, you can't design a building differently, the basic principles of getting and keeping a building 'up' are the same. Whereas in project management, you can do every aspect of it differently depending on what your attitude is, what your approach is, what your subject matter is, and how many times you've been burned before. It's way more fluid, because it is built on people and the experiences of those people.

This makes project management a very different and dynamic profession.

We have already decided, or at least we hope we have got your agreement, that project management (today) is the temporary provision of structure and transparency in order to solve short-term, complicated problems or to realise opportunities.

It sounds like a job for an extremely non-passive community of people, doesn't it?

Which, insanely, makes for an interesting dichotomy since the ownership of the project management community is seemingly drifting towards the big corporations and 'professional bodies', and yet we are not, by our inbuilt nature, an apathetic passive community. How can this be happening?

Project management is about doing stuff. It is about change. It is about being not only responsive but also proactive. 'Project manage' is a verb and not a noun. Fundamentally, it is rooted in the people doing it and those affected by it. Then how can we, as a massive multi-million worldwide community, be being led in this way?

Add to that first dichotomy a second one: we really are a special group, us project managers.

Remember, we are all about enabling others to succeed, about needing to know everything without trying, where tackling adversity and controversy is just part of the day job. We are all special. We have to be.

But, are we unique or not? Or rather, is what we do unique or not? Supposedly, we are heading towards formal professionalism and standardisation and corporate identity, and yet, conversely, what we do is non-repeatable, each change is unique, each project standing on its own and requiring an approach to suit. And the whole landscape is getting 'messier' and more challenging, project by project.

There's obviously business as usual and that's what companies do. That's what it's all about. But, effectively, there are also unusual projects, which are the big, scary, hairy beasts that are transitional stuff to beat challenges and drive strategic transformation. But then there are a whole bunch in the middle, which are projects as usual, which senior people, management, etc. all lead as part of their day job which won't be delivered in the various forms or manner of a project. All this activity and interaction is going on inside companies right now.

From the project organisation's perspective, and self-interest if we are being honest here, the world is changing and that is uncomfortable for the organisation's 'business' model (whether for profit or not).

We think it's a challenge because in some ways the world of project management we know is moving into a more decentralised collaborative and open approach.[6] This is a really good thing in general, but it feels that these organisations have worked very hard to create an 'anchor' for their members – affiliation, membership, training and certification, renewal and re-certification, standards and local engagement through meetings, as well as global gatherings. They have created the body of knowledge and therefore have the perceived sophistication and knowledge, whether rightly or wrongly, that actually means someone who wants to be 'in' has to be in some way affiliated to them, has to at the very least be a member for a period of time, and has to have gone through some form of certification and, if they want to keep it up to date/valid, keep on belonging and keep on paying.

All which says it's going to be really hard to break free.

We should all recognise that for all of the power of these organisations, such as the APM,[7] IPMA[8] and PMI[9] worldwide communities, there are still significantly way more people outside those communities in the world of project management than are actually inside it.

---

6 *The Social Project Manager: Balancing Collaboration with Centralised Control in a Project Driven World* (Gower, 2015).

7 The Association for Project Management (APM) is the chartered body for the project profession.

8 The International Project Management Association (IPMA) is a federation of about 70 Member Associations.

9 The Project Management Institute (PMI) is a global non-profit professional organization for project management, serving more than 2.9 million professionals including over 500,000 members in 208 countries and territories around the world.

And by 'way more', think millions, not thousands.

The power of the people right now says being outside is OK, being inside is fine but not necessarily required. Think optional and not mandatory.

Consideration should also be given to the 'trend'.

Five years ago, were we talking agile? We were also talking transformation. Now we are talking digital and we are talking social. The trends of project management almost require different owners. If you were delivering something that is transformational by whatever definition you choose, the trend and the ownership required for that project management skill, technique, body of knowledge, group of people is very, very different than if you're working in a strict waterfall business as usual project territory where you are just churning out a new product or a new piece of work.

It is the trend that will always influence what project management needs to be and therefore what that ownership needs to be.

Actually, what we're trying to do in the book is give everybody a bit of wiggle room within those big formal communities. In terms of who owns it, the message is we all have a responsibility to own it in that moment in time when it's yours or when it's ours. That it is, in fact, okay to almost walk alone, if only for a period of time. It's almost like dip in and dip out. That's where we rely on professional bodies to keep it consistent and to give people the opportunity to come back and disappear again.

It's almost like it's addressing apathy in project managers who do their job and say it's not their responsibility to change the methodology, to improve something, to having somebody thinking it is your responsibility because you own project management in that moment and you owe the community, so share your learning, because people are listening.

What is not bollocks is that you are 'project management' and you are the 'owner' of project management, albeit one of many; anything else is optional, and anyone who says it isn't is talking bollocks.

WHY IS NO ONE EVER TO BLAME?

"It wasn't me", stated Peter, totally not looking guilty.

"What wasn't?" questioned Susie.

"Whatever it is that has gone wrong", responded Peter nervously, "It most definitely wasn't my fault", he added for clarity.

"Unreal", said Susie, shaking her head in disbelief.

"Well that's how it goes in the wonderful world of projects I have found", argued Peter, "If you want to survive out there make sure you are never to blame and don't bother trying to find someone else to blame either, it is like a mass conspiracy".

"Exactly", Susie sighed, "nobody is ever to blame".

"It certainly seems that way", Peter agreed.

"I said that", Susie confirmed.

"Let's talk …".

Talking about 'blame' is pretty crude, but in most project failures someone or something is blamed. It might be dressed up as 'being accountable', but it's almost always played to transfer the problem and control the overspill. Name one person or event and the failure is limited, it can be 'sorted for next time'. Move on, nothing to see here anymore, all good.

Now you could argue that the lynch pin of project success is clear accountability. Bold statement, with probably a considerable amount of evidence to prove it right (one of this book's authors has written at least one book on it, so no need to go in to detail at this point, broken record and all that[10]). But this idea, or ideal, that there is a singular person within a project to protect said project from failure and to champion its success, and to provide leadership, is outdated and boring, it's really bloody boring. That a person, maybe the sponsor or possibly the project manager, becomes the scapegoat, and (unwittingly, probably) takes the blame for every minor or major misdemeanour that happens in a project's life is ridiculous (and you wonder why it's hard to get a great sponsor nowadays).

More often than not, there is never a single moment, or *force majeure* (apologies if you're reading this having been on the end of a project-limiting hurricane) that results in project failure, or substantial deviation from plan/outcome, the majority of project failure is the tragic culmination of small incremental miss-steps, whether at the first or last decision point (if you're currently in the 'failure' zone, dust yourself off, chalk it up to experience and crack on, it happens to the best of us).

So why are we in a state with heads rolling?

The glamorous answer is that there always needs to be a villain and a hero, it's the same as the movies. Someone needs to let everyone down in order for someone else to complete the rescue (enter the project hero/heroine, cape flowing, smile frighteningly white and eyes of deep blue).

But the real answer is that, as humans, we are programmed to fear failure, linked to the idea that self-worth comes from an ability to

---

10 *Strategies for Project Sponsorship* (Berrett-Koehler, 2013) by Vicki James, Ron Rosenhead and Peter Taylor.

succeed. From school age we trap ourselves in self-fulling prophecies to protect ourselves from an unsure or unwanted outcome. In the case of projects, it is to avoid being blamed. We've all done it, kept that email trail, cc'd your boss, caveated your project plan to the 'nth' degree; it's a natural human response to avoid being blamed.

So why do it?

I don't think the intention is usually to pin blame on an individual. We'll do lessons learnt, closure reports and reviews, assurance activities will pick up issues and ideas with 'owners' but we don't often find the root cause, so we see things repeated and with repetition comes frustration and with frustration comes blame. More often than not, that blame hits the top of the project pile.

Project leadership is crucial and critical, but project managers' sole purpose is not to wait for blame to fall at their feet. Their purpose should be to learn and grow, supporting those around them in doing so, in order that when a 'thing' goes 'wrong' the immediate response isn't one of finger pointing followed by the issuing of notices of employment termination. Instead, it is reflective and focused on self, giving time and space to understand and accept the outcome in order to take responsibility to move forward. There's no blame on offer here.

Project leadership from all players, all the time.

It's not just the sponsor who has a responsibility to lead. All you need is someone to follow you and you've been catapulted into the world of leadership. Being a leader is hard and messy, it needs you to balance time and patience, and practice the art of motivating a group of people to act towards achieving a common goal.

So, it is actually bollocks.

Whether you are the project sponsor, or a project support, don't spend your time looking for someone to blame (or waste time covering your arse just in case someone might try to blame you in the future).

Instead, choose to learn. Choose to hear the truth and have the courage to deal with the fall out, then move on, a better person.

DO ALL PROJECTS NEED A PROJECT MANAGER?

"When is a project not a project?" Susie asked, startling Peter.

"What are you on about now?" he responded, trying to recover his composure.

"When is a temporary endeavour undertaken to create a unique product, service or result, blah de blah just life?" Susie questioned.

"I'm confused", Peter shrugged, recognising the look in Susie's eyes that said that that happens a lot.

"OK, let me put it this way, when it is a temporary endeavour undertaken to create a unique product, service or result not delivered by a project manager", Susie declared in a confident way.

"Come again?" said Peter, giving up any pretence of non-confusion.

"Let's talk …".

This brings us back to the concept, in fact the reality, that 'projects' are in fact being delivered in more than one way, at more than one level, and by more than one community, inside organisations.

We have already stated that there are three components of organisational activity in these modern times: business as usual (of course), projects (pure and simple/complex), but also 'projects as usual' (change, managed as part of the daily work of business people who may or may not have 'project manager' in their title or even résumé).

Let's consider the value of a fully-fledged, perhaps certified, perhaps not, but definitely experienced, project manager leading a change.

They are there to lead, to own, to be at the front, to offer both vision and direction and to be the conduit to the project owner.

They are there to coordinate all communication between stakeholders and the project team, in order to bring about effective decision making and awareness.

They engage with project team members and associated subject-matter experts to define the tasks which need to be undertaken in order to complete the project.

They control the scope of the deliverables, assessing any proposed deviations for impact and value.

They control costs and coordinate resources for maximum advantage.

They consider risks as there is always a chance for potential risks to manifest themselves as issues, and a good project manager is always prepared for such eventualities.

Some even suggest that a project manager manages time but, since none are wizards or time lords and ladies, the reality is that they just keep a close eye on the clock and anticipate progress rates and define responses to any slippages.

And, of course, they are there to pay the bar bill at the end of a successful project delivery party.

But we all do those things.

Got married? Organised a big party? Sorted your kids out to go to university? Moved house? Gone on holiday? Decorated your home?

Well done, assuming it wasn't a complete balls-up then you are a manager of projects, if not a 'project manager'.

People are also doing this in the work-place, in the business world, in the industry of their choice, in their vocational activities.

They are increasingly the mistresses and masters of the art of 'getting weird stuff done'; not in a full-time way, but in a 'Can you do this alongside your day job, pretty please, as we need the change, but we really we don't need a project manager do we?' kind of way.

All this not to be confused with the unusual projects, which are the big, scary, hairy beasts that are transitional stuff that need, really need, a project manager.

So, it isn't bollocks that projects don't need project managers, in the same way that it isn't bollocks that projects always need a project manager.

What is 'bollocks' is not recognising that a project is a project even when it isn't big and scary, and the business world needs more people with the basic project delivery and change leadership skills in place, even as part of projects as usual work.

WHY ARE THERE SO MANY TWATS IN PROJECT MANAGEMENT?

"There are just so many twats in the project world", Peter declared.

"I presume you are speaking figuratively rather than literally on this one", Susie says, "If you are literal in your meaning then there may well be consequences that you will not enjoy at all".

"I'm not", Peter replied swiftly, not wanting to discover the meaning of these potential consequences.

"Good", Susie answered.

"It just seems to me, and it may well be true of many other professions, and perhaps life in general, but there are a whole bunch of twats out there in project management land", Peter continued, "and they just aren't helping anyone but themselves".

"Present company excepted, I trust?", Susie asked.

"Of course", Peter confirmed with a laugh.

"I should think so", Susie nodded.

"Let's talk …".

P robably best to start with a qualification.

If you look at any organisation, it tends to be split into many tribes, driven through role, expertise and ultimately preference. No matter how good you think your community is you will, unfortunately, rub up against folk that just aren't 'your type', running the risk that if you spend too much time with them, they'll bring out the worst in you (it will, of course, also be full of brilliant folk, so please don't assume that we are suggesting that everyone is a twat, most untrue based on our own experience of meeting and working with some great people over the years).

Here is our crude, but really quite accurate view of the 'personalities' that ripple through our communities and how to handle them.

'VOLUNTEERING ELITE'

The 'volunteering elite' are those with elevated titles such as offered by volunteer roles – president, vice-president, chairperson, director and the rest.

People choose to volunteer for a variety of reasons. For some, it offers the chance to give something back to the community or to make a difference to the people around them. For others, it provides an opportunity to develop new skills or to build on existing experience and knowledge. It can also be a positive career move by allowing them to network with a broad range of people in their business world with a wide range of connections and experience. All good stuff.

There is often the absence, in too many cases, of worthy people being up for adopting these time-consuming non-paying, evening- and weekend-taking roles, thereby creating a vacuum. And as nature abhors a vacuum, enter the volunteering elite. Not that they might actually be 'elite' in normal life, but more that they secure a role in a professional body or organisation without knowing the first thing about what that body does or supports – in our case, project management. The result being, a general annoying level of engagement and a reduced level of giving a fuck by its primary audience.

So now we know why and how to spot them, what the hell do we do about it? As with most decision points there are multiple options, but to avoid limiting your own career development and networking, or volunteering yourself (your call, there's always a risk with being apathetic), we're going with 'do nothing'; just ignore them and make some really careful choices at your next meeting, conference or networking event.

'FIRST LOSER GANG'

Second place goes to the 'first loser gang' (all together now: 'I wouldn't have done it that way'), you know the types – 'My project is bigger than yours, quicker than yours'; 'I have more qualifications than I even know what to do with'; 'This one time … when I was asked to save the day, and do it single handed, with only a budget of £8 and an old cheese sandwich'.

These folks are probably the worst view of our profession, because with this overt competition tends to come some form of belittling, or passive aggressive tone. It's not fun and it's not healthy, but we are sure you can think of at least one example (although, if you are completely honest, I'm sure you've been that person too at some point – think on).

Whilst there's no space for nasty, this sort of 'person of a twattish nature' tends to come from a place of exposure, where the individual feels exposed in a way that feels hard and is probably quite unhappy. There's usually a bit of baggage, maybe they've been burnt, or overlooked. But it still sucks, it's still royally miserable to be on the receiving end.

So how do you take them down? The answer to this one is, you don't. Fighting fire with fire isn't going to address the problem; instead, bridge the gap to curb their behaviour. Now it's time to dig deep and counteract their behaviour with your own, so role model the relationships you'd like, and demonstrate how to support colleagues and peers through sharing ideas, exploring options and working through it, together. Show that friendly competition can drive greater learning, and higher knowledge transfer creates a community that can grow and evolve together, better and faster. On this one, you just need to be the better person.

All that being said, the day you close the deal, deliver the project or win the trophy, sing and shout about it. But do it gracefully, or at least try.

'GANG LEADERS' AND 'TRIBES'

Next are the 'gang leaders' – we're thinking less mobster and more 'Do you want to be in my gang?'. These can be slippery little fishes, as they sneak up on you when you least expect it, and you might not know it's happened until it's too late, because they too are just 'going about their business' in the environment that we created ourselves.

Linked to this there are 'Tribes'. More nuanced, 'their tribes'.

Tribes are created within project management, like every other part of business life. You pick a tribe when you choose a methodology, a thought process or a professional body, or you hear an idea and it sparks an interest, and then you become committed; the gang leader sees your commitment and – 'KAPOW' – you are speaking at conferences, facilitating workshops, speed dating, having coffee, doing almost anything other than what got you interested in your tribe in the first place, with an overwhelming feeling of 'stop the bus, I want to get off'.

So how to deal?

Now this is sink or swim. The relationship of being in with a gang leader, no matter how much of a twat they are (or become), will quite often sway how you actually tackle some of the stuff that you were trying to do, achieve or challenge through providing you with a platform or partnership from which to start, and sometimes you need help in doing, in order to prove that you can or should. So, in these cases, take the help, drink the coffee and run with it. At the point where this relationship hits the 'twat-ometer', press the eject button, leave the WhatsApp group, and just bail.

Do it with pride … and do it with style, don't be an arse.

So, is it bollocks?

Yes, it is. But is it worth arguing about? Nah.

We're minded to just accept that there just are, and more than likely always will be, twats in project management (as in every other aspect of work and life, if we are honest about it). This stance may well bring you to a point of serenity and grace or we might have just pointed out enough flaws in the human psyche to distract you beyond useful.

If that is the case, then totally soz. But if you've taken the time (or you take the time in the future, we're not in the market for instant reward) to reflect on your approach, behaviour or attitude, our work here is done. Be the person you needed when you were growing up, when your last project was going wrong or when you celebrated your big success. Be that person: the profession, colleagues and those who come after you will thank you for it.

THE CONCLUSION

We trust that the conclusion at this point is so blatantly obvious it is barely worth our while writing it down. But we will anyway. Just in case you skipped to this part.

You are project management – project management is yours – don't be a twat about it – many activities in life can use your skills – make sure you are clear on your identity – do not, under any circumstances, piss around with the 'blame game' – and, in the words of Richard Branson (and The Sex Pistols[11]), 'Never mind the bollocks'.

---

11 'Never Mind the Bollocks, Here's the Sex Pistols' is the only studio album by English punk rock band the Sex Pistols, released on 28 October 1977 by Virgin Records. The album has influenced many bands and musicians, and the industry in general. In particular, the album's raw energy, and Johnny Rotten's sneering delivery and 'half-singing' are often considered game-changing. It is frequently listed as the most influential punk album, and one of the most important albums of all time.

The Question Isn't Who Is Going To Let Me – It's Who Is Going To Stop Me?

Attributed: Ayn Rand

CHAPTER TWO

Seven cracking ideas

Here the authors will offer a selection of cracking ideas, that when applied to a project environment will ultimately result in you being a good manager of projects in this modern world of business complexity and 'everything needed yesterday but hey, don't forget your day job'.

THE PREMISE

As we have explored, right now, there is a growth in 'projects as usual' – something somewhere in between full on, full out major project change and everyday business as usual that is the core of any organisation. There remain 'projects as projects' of course, and everything we cover here applies in that pure project world as well, but for those 'projects as usual' folks out there, what we aim to cover are the absolute key basics.

Our starting point for this is to recognise that project life is certainly not 'painting by numbers', but most certainly does not need a big volume of project mantra jargon to justify its existence. This, maybe, does have a use in propping open your office door (unless you have already won an award, as one, but not the other, of the authors has so done).

What we all do need is some bloody good common sense and a few basics of understanding, which is exactly what we aim to deliver in this chapter.

We are calling it the 'seven cracking ideas to make project management better'; snappy title, I'm sure you will agree. Well, it has to be called something, and that was the best that we could come up with, and since we don't have the support of a mega marketing department with a bunch of brand managers,[1] let's accept this one and move swiftly on. It will suffice.

If you remember, from the opening words of the book, we consider this to be the really useful chapter, the one where we filter out all the crap, distil the good down to the bare minimum, the essential elements if you like, and present the seven key principles of being an effective project manager in the modern world of getting weird shit done. This is the bit you don't want to read late at night when tired, or on the tube when you are too distracted, or when the kids have decided that now is the time to try to engage you in parent interaction, but at a time when you can really consider what we are saying and how this might well apply to yourself.

---

1 This is a totally gratuitous place to mention another book by one of this book's authors: *Project Branding: Using Marketing to Win the Hearts and Minds of Stakeholders* by Peter Taylor (RMC Publications, 2014).

It is for your own good after all.

Trust us, we are professionals.

Added to that, as promised, we have aimed to do this in the best possible taste and with the intention of bringing a realistic understanding to current and future practitioners of change delivery about what it means to be a project manager today, next Tuesday and the future even beyond that.

If you remember, the very title of this book *Project Management: It's all Bollocks!* gave a strong hint on the path that we're following. You have had the 'bollocks', and now we get down to the nitty gritty part of project management.

So, hold on to your hats, make sure you have a clean set of underwear, take a firm grip of whatever is close to hand, and let's go.

CRACKING IDEA 1: EVERYTHING IS A SURPRISE

S URPRISE!

Fail to plan and prepare to fail they say. Well, Benjamin Franklin supposedly once said, 'If you fail to plan, you are planning to fail', and Sir Winston Churchill is credited with another, oft repeated, saying: 'Those who fail to learn from the past are doomed to repeat it'.

Nice idea, but even the best planners get caught short.

Dealing with change means dealing with uncertainty and as most change involves people at some point, what you're actually trying to do is to herd cats, whilst under attack from an over enthusiastic puppy.[2]

You'll never think of it all. That's fine. A project manager can't know everything. A business case can't think of everything. A sponsor really is not some omnipresent deity, even though at times you wish that they were.

A plan can't account for everything.

'Everything', in our business just doesn't exist, so stop fooling yourself that it does. Even projects that use fancy tools and even fancier techniques for risk management or planning can encounter extremely surprising outcomes (to put it politely).

Those techniques, while super powerful, can only manage what we know. We know the projects are new and unique, operating in environments that are ambiguous (and slightly bonkers), so why don't we stop pretending that a plan can save us and instead get ready for the volatile and ambiguous world that we are actually operating in.

Let's be bold and brave and embrace the change, or the surprise.

We are always told how important planning is, you know how it goes: 'The Seven Ps – Proper, Prior, Planning, Prevents, Piss, Poor, Performance'.

We guess there is a point here; however, not knowing your tolerances and priorities is likely to cause you more bother. So, you plan, using your best endeavours, you follow advice and reference lessons learnt, you ask others and you gain consensus, or as much as you can. Result: you have the 'bestest' plan ever. But you didn't ask 'Why?' You didn't

---

2 To be completely clear, no metaphorical animals were harmed in the writing of this book.

understand the problem properly and now you're heading off in the wrong direction, or to the wrong drumbeat.

And then we're told that risk management will prevent surprises, but there's still a casual chorus of 'we didn't see that coming' around the steering group table. That's because we don't have crystal balls, we don't have access to foresight, we can only learn from what we've done and from where we've been, which is great, but some days it won't be good enough. So, what can you do about it?

Project knowledge and insight come from learning about the project – its purpose, the environment it is operating in, its goals and objectives, the people affected, the resources available to you and the role, and the experience of your sponsor. This is, admittedly, complicated but it is working out how all of these affect one another that is key.

Understanding begins at the planning stage, where you really get under the hood of the project. But you need to actually do it; more often than not a project is approved and, all of a sudden, we're buying things and hiring people (and heaven forbid, making commitments, whether actual or assumed), before we've given ourselves enough time, at the right time, to evaluate options and unpick risks. Why? Because we're excited (like that room full of puppies), we're ready and, more than that, we know it all (however, the gap knowable about a project and what is actually known can be quite whopping!). Enter surprise.

We all know, you don't know what you don't know.[3] It's not rocket science (well it could be, but we don't necessarily know).

---

3 A fun take on this concept is the quote from the ex-United States Secretary of Defense, Donald Rumsfeld, who stated: 'Reports that say that something hasn't happened are always interesting to me, because as we know, there are known knowns; there are things we know we know. We also

Anyhow, it's how we respond to this that's really important. If there are things we don't know, but we know that our knowledge or experience doesn't leap that far, we can consciously combat it, through bringing in expertise or knowledge. It gets dangerous when you aren't open to the possibility that you 'don't know', which is where we lose awareness and/or ignore gaps in our own knowledge. It's an unconscious absence and exposes us on many fronts. Enter surprise.

Many surprises aren't really surprising at all. In fact, you could easily argue that the only real surprise in a project is if there were no surprises. That would indeed be surprising. Rather, they are things that no one has bothered to find out about. At the end of the day, you're only ever right or wrong in hindsight, so just be prepared to be surprised.

Of course, you should be consciously hunting out new insight, seeking new advice and asking for more guidance early and often. When the surprise does land, don't sit there looking busy, furiously checking Facebook or job hunting, take the time to reflect and to learn both in the moment and in the calm that follows.

CRACK ON 1

Starting right now, understand and accept that everything is a surprise – which means, by simple deduction, you need to get prepared for being surprised at every opportunity that life can find to surprise you:

---

know there are known unknowns; that is to say we know there are some things we do not know. But there are also unknown unknowns – the ones we don't know we don't know'.

1. Work out what good looks like, some surprises will add value to what you do, others will take you to a very dark place. Know how to differentiate them, quickly and accurately.

2. Learn to be OK with the plan always changing and accept help when it comes to planning. Most project managers are good at planning, but they aren't 'great' at investing your time or your money in a 'planning expert' whether to write it, re-write it or test it, use scenarios, understand cause and effect of impact and that sort of thing. This will help you build a bit of resilience for when the surprises start rolling in.

3. Start running into rooms and shouting 'SURPRISE'. People won't like it, but it might mean they think twice before they do it to you.

INSPIRATION – THE MARKER PEN SYNDROME

Peter says:

The question that is often asked amongst many of us in project management is 'Why didn't we learn from that experience?'

Albert Einstein said 'Insanity is doing the same thing over and over again and expecting different results'.[4]

So why do we accept 'insanity' as the path of project management?

The next time you are in a meeting, just try this out. Whether you are presenting or someone else is doesn't matter, but what happens when

---

4 Apparently, he didn't say that. We've all heard Albert Einstein's famous line: 'Insanity is doing the same thing over and over again and expecting different results'. But it seems he never spoke those words. Sorry to disappoint and sorry about all the inspirational posters, mugs, placemats, aprons and t-shirts that might have to be binned now. That said, it is a truth and it is, therefore, a great quote.

the inevitable happens – you go to write something on the flip chart, or the whiteboard, and the pen is dry? How many of you (and I freely admit I am just as guilty) put the pen down on the rack again, pick up another one and carry on with the key, interesting, important point you were making, thereby leaving the same dry pen for the next person – or worse, for yourself – to do the same thing again a little later in the meeting (yes, been there, done that)?

Did you expect the pen to magically refill itself? Of course not, madness!

Did you put the pen in the bin and ensure that a new one was put in its place, or at least noted for someone that new pens were required? Of course not, madness!

A simple lesson in lessons learned or, to be more precise, the process of not learning.

Does this mean that, somehow, we are programmed to not learn lessons?

Clearly not, since if that was the case then we would have wiped ourselves out as a race a long, long, long time ago.

So why don't we learn lessons when it comes to project experiences?

Well I think that in actual fact we do, or personally we do. Our personal project experience has to be a learning experience (even if that learning experience is 'I am getting out of project management and finding a real job to do …').

No, we do learn, and we do progress and grow as project managers and we are all the better for it.

The challenge comes from sharing the knowledge of those lessons amongst others, and from learning from others' experience in return.

It is a matter of scale and capability all mixed in with time and priorities.

It is not the process of binning the empty pen and replacing the pen, but in letting others know what you did and why you did it, how it can benefit them in the future and why they should also pass on this piece of knowledge.

It is less about 'lessons learned' and more about 'lessons shared'.

So, the next time you go to write something on the flipchart, or the whiteboard, and the pen is dry, stop – turn to face your audience and say 'Right this pen is going in the bin and let me tell you why …'.

Because the next time you plan the unknown then at least you will have one more known to not have to worry about.

CRACKING IDEA 2: FAILURE IS AN OPTION

Appreciating that failure is an option, as long as you just make sure you learn from the experience and don't fuck up twice in the same way, is the secret to living, learning and generally make solid progress.

Fail fast, learn quick, do not repeat. Sounds easy.

The bollock test here is do you really believe that success is the only plausible, or anticipated outcome? That everyone around you, your peers, your stakeholders, your management, do not (and perhaps do not on a regular basis) screw it up somehow? That you must, really must, absolutely must, get it right every single time?

No. We didn't think so. That way madness lies.

Failure is the state or condition of not meeting a desirable or intended objective, and may be viewed as the opposite of success, but then again, it can also (occasionally) be the platform for unexpected success,[5] and it can always be the basis for future success.

You can definitely overdose on stimulating quotes on this subject, 'Success is not final, failure is not fatal: it is the courage to continue that counts', Winston Churchill for example; 'Failures, repeated failures, are finger posts on the road to achievement. One fails forward toward success', C. S. Lewis; and one more for the road 'There are no secrets to success. It is the result of preparation, hard work, and learning from failure', Colin Powell. OK, enough, you get the picture.

Failure is an option.

For some people and therefore projects, failure ruins them, taking them to a point of no return. For others (probably a minority in the project world), it can be the beginning of something brilliant. But to achieve brilliance you also need to fail and own the failure. Which is easier said than done.

There are two distinct avenues for failure and it's the path we choose that determines whether failure curses us or becomes an asset:

- *Owning it*: when we royally 'balls up', staking claim to the failure with clear accountability, ownership, and probably an apology, can act like one of life's best teachers. We shake ourselves off, learn from our mistakes and move on.
- *Shifting the blame*: notably the most common, and sometimes the most preferred option it has to be said, but there's definitely less

---

5 Examples of this commonly shared include Edison's 10,000 attempts to create a light bulb or Dyson's 5,126 attempts to invent a bagless vacuum cleaner.

joy from this option and a much slower recovery. When we make excuses for ourselves, blame the context, environment or even another person, we're actively avoiding the consequences of our actions, the results are the opposite, we don't learn, we don't grow and more than likely we'll hit more failures pretty soon (and you'll probably look like a massive wazzock).

When our response to failure is ignorance or avoidance, to the point when failing is failure in itself (this could get confusing but stay with us on this one) we, and therefore our projects, are less likely to recover and it becomes even more unlikely that we'll learn from it and increasingly likely that we'll repeat it.

We can only receive what failure has to teach us if we're willing to fully embrace the failure itself. When you're willing to accept the fact that failure occurred, you also get the positive lessons failure teaches.

Failure can feel like utter shite, especially the big, or public types. We are not trying to encourage you to have failure love-ins where you share terrible stories and forgive each other in some sort of weird cult-type scenario, gathered in the circle of trust or some other such bollocks, but where we are trying to take you to is a point of acceptance.

Learning from failure prevents further failure. This is a good thing and you'll probably get the result you want (second time round).

CRACK ON 2

Fail fast, learn quick, and do your best to not repeat the same mistake.

Job done.

1. Break it all down into bite size components, deliverables, tasks, etc., 'big bang' is your enemy when it comes to failure-proof points.
2. Make sure you have in place a mechanism that suits your style, and that of your team, in order to learn the lessons in a fast and furious but constructive way.
3. And if you feel a bout of repetition coming on then stop, pause, regroup, get help, and don't panic.

Fail; Learn; Succeed; Repeat. Go buy the t-shirt and crack on.

INSPIRATION – THE ONE AT THE INTERVIEW

Susie says:

Not having the years that Peter has[6] I can't just whip out a quick parable about a single man who slayed a giant, having reflected on his failings and improved his outcomes, but I can tell you about a time where I was called out on my own failure and what it made me realise.

I was interviewing for a pretty whopping job, to be fair I was probably punching above my weight but that's never stopped me before.

I was asked, in a room full of people, to give an example as to when I had contributed to a project (full/partial) failure and what I had learnt from it. Fine. I'm cool with that. Cue next part of the question. I was given two choices, I could go with an example of where the organisation construct had caused the failure and I wasn't in a position to succeed due to said limitations, or I could give an example where

---

6 Peter: She has to get the 'ageist' dig in at every opportunity …

my individual actions had resulted in failure. Shit. They actually want me to confess to fucking something up. Bastards!

Fine, here we go. So, I whipped the plaster off and explained the situation and how me not doing something (in this case, speaking up more often and louder against something I didn't believe in) contributed to the demise of a pretty massive programme of works. It felt good. I realised that I was ultimately OK with my actions and I had learnt and continued to learn what the course of action meant for me in a project role, a position of leadership and as a human.

What surprised me was the reaction of the panel. Their faces said it all.

They were not OK with my failure; they were literally imploding with questions that were coming at me fast and furious. That was a lesson, or a point of validation, that leaders are often those most fearful of failure, both their own and those who surround them. Although a pretty big ask, it's actually our job to take our leaders through our own, the project's, the organisation's failings in a way that's supported and forward focused, because failure hits people differently and if you're responsible for steering the ship, it's really good to be told the ship's taking on water in good time and preferably with a solution already in motion.

I didn't get the job. I don't think it was because of that question, I had many more questionable responses to the interview, culminating in me referring to a group of stakeholders as 'awkward sods'. They weren't my people. I wasn't their person. Lesson learnt.

So, take from this what you want, or need. But if you take anything, chill out when it comes to failure, take time to recover and go again. And probably the best bit, you can still get a book deal if you fuck up an interview. This is the proof.

CRACKING IDEA 3: COMMUNICATION VERSUS ENGAGEMENT – CHOOSE WISELY OR LIVE WITH THE CONSEQUENCE

First off, there is a fundamental difference between communication and engagement.

Communication, in its most literal sense, is what to say and who to say it to. It is more distant, identified at arm's length. Engagement is more hands on, identifying who to listen to, what feedback you seek to elicit and then getting that feedback.

Think of it this way: communication is one-way, usually broadcast information, narrative or key messages are pushed up, out and away.

It is when this communication is supported or enabled into being a conversation, something that is two-way, where answers are sought and listened to, that we're now hitting engagement.

The more common type of communication (not that we are agreeing that this is, in fact, communication as such) is along the lines of you having a meeting, a call, slamming together an email, popping out an SMS or doing whatever you do, in whichever way you do it, and all you end up doing is 'pushing' what you want to say to whoever you want to say it to.

Result, communication in play, failure to engage.

Or you put together a wondrous piece of advanced art that is a multi-page, mega fact including, multi-coloured visually appealing masterpiece that you call a 'status report', and you send it to everyone you have ever met.

Result, communications dispatched, failure to engage, with a possible bonus of pissing off some people completely with your attitude.

What we're getting at is the idea or truth; that communication in isolation of engagement or just without it, will lead to dead ends.

As we said, engagement is a two-way process. You are communicating out and you are receiving something back, and the usual complexities of filters and noise typically confuse the process of giving and receiving clear, accurate and understandable information. Assumptions are made, misunderstandings arise, lack of attention contributes to errors in 'translation' and Chinese whispers ensue.

We all know this. We have all suffered as a result (and sometimes benefitted as well). We are all guilty. Don't bother trying to deny this to yourself, you know it is true.

Engagement (good) (effective) (useful) happens only when you have the magic combination of right information delivered in the right way to the right person and at the right time.

And then you support the recipient in doing something useful with it, and you wait, encourage and receive their response. Now, what you choose to listen to and act on is, of course, entirely your choice.

This point is that you need to choose wisely when you devise your communications strategy, being conscious that communication in insolation of defined and purposeful engagement will only get you so far. Engagement builds on communications, they complement each other and are proven to increase satisfaction and generate 'buy-in', projects that really understand the what, how, when, why and who of communication will probably experience more joy in the medium of happier, more interested and cooperative stakeholders and teams.

And that's bloody super.

CRACK ON 3

Communication strategies include everything from an email to a town hall event. When we talk *just* communications, we're thinking broadcast not dialogue. We've skirted over some broad-brush definitions but there are heaps of academic and professional texts about the art of communication, how to engage people properly in order to secure success, etc. Rather than ploughing through 64,000 articles on Google Scholar, we reckon it's actually far simpler than we're led to believe.

1. Understand what it is you want to say and why, and whether you're actually interested in a response (sometimes it's OK to not care, so consciously acknowledge that you're heading for broadcast communications not engagement).
2. Identify whether you need a response, what that response might look like and the steps you'll need to take to help people return that response.
3. Understand your audience and their level of interest, put the effort in to the supporters and the 'not quite sures' rather than flogging yourself in an attempt to win over the 'haters'.
4. Speak the same language, consistently and over time.
5. Ask for help, advocates from within key stakeholder groups are your strongest allies and can often be more powerful than you banging on about the supposedly important stuff. They know how to tailor their message, already understand any concerns and know how to handle the troublemakers.
6. And remember, more often than not you have to give something to get something (it's that kind of world).

The saying goes 'you can't be everyone's cup of tea, if you were then you'd be a mug'.

The same goes for project engagement and communication (and engagement). No matter what you do or aspire to be, it won't land well with everyone, you'll miss the mark and you'll miss entire groups of people. So, keep it simple, make conscious decisions and remember it's OK to get it wrong, shake yourself off and go again.

INSPIRATION – BANGERS AND MASH

Peter says:

Now if you are from the UK you will 100% know what I am talking about, and if you are from Canada, Australia or New Zealand (I am reliably informed) you will also have a good chance of knowing what 'bangers and mash' are. But if you are from elsewhere and haven't had the personal pleasure of enjoying a mouthful of 'bangers and mash' (tasty) then you are probably completely confused.

For the record, 'bangers and mash', also known as sausages and mash, is a traditional British dish made up of mashed potatoes and (typically) fried sausages.

The sausage part (or 'banger') may consist of a variety of sausage flavours made of pork or beef or a perhaps even a Cumberland sausage (if you are being posh), and the dish is sometimes served with onion gravy, fried onions, baked beans, or peas, preferably – in my personal case with 'mushy peas'. And so, we are off again aren't we? You have no idea what mushy peas are do you? Sorry, go look it up on the world wide web of wonder.

Why 'banger' we hear you ask? Well, the term is attributed to the fact that sausages made during World War I, when there were meat shortages, were made with such a high water content that they were very liable to pop under high heat when cooked. Modern day sausages don't have this attribute, they just sizzle, delightfully so.

One of the authors wrote an article a while ago on 'The Business of Meaningless Words', about the growth in bland, tired and need-to-be retired clichés, but there is another aspect to such 'code' that isn't meaningless and still needs to be known, or translated, in order to communicate efficiently.

'Bangers and mash' for example is not shorthand for 'sausages and mash' but rather an alternative term, colloquial, perhaps even slang, but still, if you say, started work in an English pub, that both served good beer and 'pub grub' food, then you would need to know what it was for sure. I'd be in there ordering it!

PMI's White Paper on Communication states *'Communication is what allows projects – and the organization – to function efficiently. Conversely, when key players at any level fail to deliver their end of the communication bargain, projects face unnecessary risks'.*[7]

And one of the levels of failure can be in not explaining terms to people who do not know them and, here's the balance, asking what terms mean if you don't know them or understand their meaning.

See what I did there? Communication is a two-way responsibility. Explain, and give time for clarity, don't assume understanding; and then ask, challenge and seek clarity; don't fake understanding.

Got it? Excellent.

---

7 PMI, *Communication: The Message is Clear* (PMI White Papers, 2013).

Right I'm off for a quick bevvy and fancying a nice plate of bubble and squeak for supper with perhaps a chip butty on the side.[8]

How about you?

CRACKING IDEA 4: ENGAGE THE WILLING, WORK WITH THE ABLE AND DEAL WITH THE REST LATER

E ngage the willing and work with the able.

What we are talking about is some good old-fashioned stakeholder management. What's not to love? Other than everything that is.

Life would be simple without people, right?

Who presents you with the most challenges, questions and hurdles?

People.

What is the most important thing to have in a project?

People.

Why do most projects fail?

People. (They never say that on the myriad of surveys and research articles published year after year about the endless stories of project failure, but in the end, people fuck it all up – you know that right?)

---

8 You have no idea what they are either do you? Again, go look it up on the world wide web of wonder.

The trouble is that people bring complexities like bears shit in the woods, and people are literally everywhere. But now it's time to work out how to get the right folk lifting you up and how to shake off the rest.

To be honest, there's nothing 'old fashioned' about our new ideas for stakeholder management. We are whipping the plaster off and just saying it out loud. Some people are better for your project than others. What we're talking about you won't find in a RACI,[9] you definitely won't find it in a stakeholder map and it's not driven by who has the purse strings.

Some people will help your project win and others will feel like they are little blocks of concrete holding on to your ankles making everything feel shite.

Let's talk about those who'll help you succeed. We call these the willing.

They are willing because they might like your project, or idea, they may want to try to fix the same thing you want to fix, and they are usually firm believers that the paradigm of 'we are where we are' is bollocks and that we should be aiming to get to places that are better, less 'bollocky' if you like. Which is glorious, blinking marvellous and singlehandedly changes the forces within a project.

The able are those with the skills or knowledge you really need.

They can get you places, unlocking the next level in your project so you can build momentum, design solutions that actually work and

---

9 Lord help us if, dear reader, you don't know what a RACI is, but just in case (because we really are inclusive people after all) – simply, a RACI describes the participation by various roles in completing tasks or deliverables for a project. RACI is an acronym derived from the four key responsibilities most typically used: Responsible, Accountable, Consulted, and Informed.

deliver your change in a way that can be understood and received. They are the ones who bring subject matter expertise, those who let you into their networks, those to lean on or learn from others. They have a wealth of knowledge, ideas and ability. You need them. You need to find them, and you need to embed them with the 'willing'.

Do that and together you have rocket fuel, with the power of the willing and the able standing behind you and your project, helping you to succeed.

Not bad eh?

The acquisition of the willing and the able should be relatively straightforward, so we will leave you to sort that out, but now it is time to deal with 'the rest later' group of people.

This is a simple lesson; people are people and that means they are busy/bored/don't like you or your project/crazy/difficult/deviant and much more besides. Sometimes through no fault of their own (genetics, breeding, nurture) and sometimes because they are consciously just being sodding awkward.

Some are apathetic, but some are doing cooler stuff than you. They are not in your gang and they aren't coming.

So, the bit that's bollocks is trying to work within traditional expectations of stakeholder management, when projects haven't been 'traditional' as much as they have been delivered 'in a controlled environment'. Identify the types of people you need, think bigger and broader than what you've been encouraged to do before. Look for personalities, glimmers in eyes, a beaming smile at the end of a bright idea. Look for the diamonds in the rough, find the people who have passion and skill, and let them help you deliver and succeed.

CRACK ON 4

So how do we find what we're looking for and how far do we go trying to muster up converts?

There are several steps:

1. As noted, find those with a glimmer in their eye when you talk about a project or problem. They'll be great to have on board.
2. Talk to folk about who might be interested or have the skill set you need. Then set about 'poaching them' (not as in illegal killing of animals poaching, more acquiring and distracting their skill from what it is they should be doing).
3. Share ideas and open yourself to new ideas, you'll surface powerful catalysts and capabilities if you are open and willing to others.
4. As for the rest, you can start off begging and pleading to encourage them to join a formidable force of 'willing and able' or move on, let them be. Share your ideas in ways that are accessible, be clear on the implications that they might experience, but, in the words of Elsa,[10] let it go. Nobody needs that level of grief.

INSPIRATION – CREATING SOMETHING FROM NOTHING

Susie says:

We knew that we needed to tackle an ongoing problem within a large organisation (if I tell you the problem, I'll probably end up in front of the FBI or at least in massive trouble with my mum, so we'll just refer to it as the 'problem').

---

10 Elsa, *Frozen*, Disney – enough said.

The issue was that the problem felt too hard and complicated to form a team to fix.

So rather than setting up a task group to 'resolve' the said 'problem' we started a conversation about what could be different. We did it in coffee shops and at the end of meetings, and we kept going until more and more people were talking about the problem (N.B. it was a calculated starting of conversations, not just a cool outcome following a cup of tea and a scone).

These conversations led to small groups making changes, tiny iterative steps and contributions towards solving the problem.

The ripple effects of the able and willing became really evident until 'everyone else' was aware of the movement, change of tide, new culture that was emerging around them. The ripple turned into a wave, the wave brought many hands, ideas and voices that were all focused on solving the 'problem'.

The 'problem' started to feel easier. The 'problem' became less of a problem. And it was no longer clear who was able, willing or otherwise because we were finally all marching to the same drumbeat.

'Problem' resolved.

CRACKING IDEA 5: THERE IS NEVER A SINGLE POINT OF FAILURE

Realising that there is never a single point of failure is essential in this world of change delivery – so ignore all the surveys out there because they won't help you. Really, they won't.

You know the ones. They come out regularly from all the major authorities, the project communities and associations, the big consultancy boys and girls, the major trend evaluators, and anyone who fancies a bit of a headline (and PR).

Just go search for 'project failure' and you will have enough reading to last a lifetime.

But assuming that you have better uses of your time, let's go back to single points of failure, which is a part of a system that, if it fails, will stop everything from working. A bit like running out of fuel, the car is perfectly functioning but you ain't going anywhere fast (or even slow).

Projects are not like that. Projects are complicated beasts for sure in some cases, and there may be particular stress points that could cause failure but, mostly, failure is a whole set of cumulative teeny tiny things that occur along the way.

They all add up. Accumulate. Grow in significance until 'bam' you're down and out. Failure has occurred.

OK, maybe there are single points of risk – the old 'red bus' taking out your key subject matter expert on the M25 or Thor the hammer-wielding god of thunder striking your entire server farm, but these are biggies and can, and should, be considered, and mitigation planned.

Aside from these then the rest is a slow accumulation of errors, miscommunication, assumptions badly made, and decisions (or indecisions) taken (or not taken).

As a result of this reality check, take a good look at the recent history of your project and consider what and how this is tracking now.

Build in your tracking of progress, your iterative lessons learned points, your objective reviews of how you got here, why you are here and where you were supposed to be instead. Learn from your project and the people who sit within it. Understand when your gut feeling of 'something's not right' is actually a telling indicator of where you are (rather than what you have eaten). The use of tracking, both the project outcomes and the sentiment that surrounds your project is a pretty solid system of levers and widgets that can alert to you minor misdemeanour or growing 'gotcha' moments.

CRACK ON 5

Starting with the acceptance that there is never a single point of failure is critical.

1. That said, there can be binary and actual single points of potential failure, so consider these carefully at the start of the project. Then plan some great mitigation. And don't forget to ask the question 'Is it me?'
2. That done, move on to the far more likely scenario by making sure you don't create a perceived single point of failure by letting a whole bunch of tiddlers get together and form a great big pool of trouble.

It is about anticipation and about small corrective actions along the way.

INSPIRATION – JUMPING THE SHARK

Peter says:

The usage of 'jump the shark' identifies the moment when a brand, a design, a franchise, a creative effort, or anything reaches a point when it becomes something unwelcome, unpleasant or unwarranted.

The phrase derives from a scene in a Season 5 episode of the 1970s sitcom 'Happy Days'[11] in which the character Fonzie jumps over a shark while on water-skis. This ridiculous gimmick was so absurdly outside the original storyline of the sitcom that it became the stuff of (negative) legend.

In the project world the phrase could well be that moment when your 'failure' is squarely and uncomfortably in the spotlight of realisation within your organisation. The point when there is nowhere left to hide the failure and nowhere left to run either. It is there for all to see – to stare and point, to laugh or to look slightly relieved that they weren't carrying the parcel when the bomb went off.

Naturally, one way to avoid your very own personal 'shark' moment is to not reach that point of failure, but maybe step (carefully) over some small goldfish on a regular basis instead. You know when I mean. Don't wait for it all to blow up and become crazy bad. Keep looking back, keep checking on progress to plan (well progress to that point of anticipated success). Assess often and regularly. Keep it real and keep it under control.

To be fair to the 'Happy Days' analogy, the producers did point out that the episode in question had a viewing figure of over 30 million (very respectable in the United States) and that the series went on for another six seasons (way longer than most modern sitcoms), so it wasn't fatal, even though the 'jumping the shark' phrase went on to become an industry classic.

---

11 'Happy Days' was an American television sitcom that aired from January 15, 1974 to September 24, 1984 on ABC, starring Ron Howard as teenager Richie Cunningham, Henry Winkler as his friend Arthur 'Fonzie' or 'The Fonz' Fonzarelli, and Tom Bosley and Marion Ross as Richie's parents, Howard and Marion Cunningham.

Perhaps the moral of this is that even if you have reached the point of (multiple) failure then all is not lost. Even the worst situation is often recoverable from. Even when the sharks might be circling.

CRACKING IDEA 6: YOU DON'T NEED TO BE EMPOWERED AND YOU DON'T NEED PERMISSION

Here comes the science.

Empowerment originated within the organisational science sphere; it was a term used to cover a number of activities that can affect how a worker performs. In its simplest form empowerment was understood as a form of motivation. But we are not going to go to town on motivational theory (there's plenty out there on the world wide web of wonder).

Instead, we want to strip it from our projects, our offices and our conversations, because no matter how you dress it up, waiting to be empowered is just going to leave you waiting and wanting.

Right now, in our organisations and workplaces, when we use the word 'empower', and more to the point when we are wanting or waiting to be empowered, more often than not we are actually focused on the (em)power.

We are in search of more, or different power, than what we currently have. But power isn't infinite or renewable in the business sense, so we arrive at a more literal understanding of empower – that is to give power to (someone); to make (someone) stronger and more confident. So, this search for empowerment implies that you are in some way lacking, that you need permission, influence or talent, etc. from somewhere or someone else to achieve your outcomes.

The same can be said for those who seek permission.

The need for permission comes from a place where you feel you don't have the authority or credibility. But being given permission won't build your credibility, what will is actually doing the job, achieving the goal, and having courageous conversations. Being given permission within a project, doesn't make the project successful, doesn't make the outcomes right and doesn't make delivery easier.

Seeking permission and waiting for empowerment aren't getting you anywhere fast and it's certainly no fun. But the signals you're sending come down to one pretty rough point, that ultimately, without them, you don't think you're good enough.

Ouch!

OK, maybe that's a little harsh, you are good enough, you're just not applying what's already in your gift very well, or consistently to achieve the outcomes that you're searching for. Or you're not digging what you're working on, there are no sparks, the fire in your belly has gone out, you are just committed. And right now, we've done a full loop back to empowerment as a form of motivator.

Casual segue into the renowned Frederick Herzberg,[12] who has spent a long time exploring and exploding many motivational theories. If we bring together two schools of thought on empowerment and

---

12 Frederick Irving Herzberg (1923–2000) was an American psychologist who became one of the most influential names in business management. He is most famous for introducing job enrichment and the Motivator-Hygiene theory describing factors for satisfaction (motivators/satisfiers) and factors for dissatisfaction (hygiene factors/dissatisfiers).

motivation, the need for and the expectation to be given – this supports the claim that it is not your manager's responsibility to motivate (read empower) you, but it is their responsibility to create an environment where each of your individual sparks can burn brightly.

An environment where you can flourish.

CRACK ON 6

Rather than waiting to be empowered, or for someone to give you permission, approach projects (and life) focusing on:

1. Finding your place in your project's vision or objectives. Seek clarity until it feels right, until it provides an anchor.
2. Creating space for reflection, creativity and getting your hands dirty. Get to grips with what you're trying to achieve and then achieve it.
3. Seeking out opportunities to make connections and build a sense of professional identify and credibility. And help others to do so too.

Stop waiting. Start doing. Deliver value. Enjoy your work. Learn new things. Be the best version of you. Stop standing around sipping coffee waiting for the power truck to come. It isn't coming. So don't wait for it.

INSPIRATION – BE YOUR OWN POSTCARD

Susie says:

This is our pep talk for you. The one you can read when it all feels shitty. It's pretty short, so read it twice.

We all love those postcards, I bet you have one in your diary or stuck to your fridge. You know the ones I mean, the ones you see at the train station when you feel a bit shitty and they tell you in a single snappy sentence that you're great, just the way you are, or that it doesn't matter if you're old and fat because all your mates are too. The principles of these are simple. They are basically telling you to pull yourself together and go and win at life. And they are telling you to do it, because nobody can do it for you. And we agree (with each other and the rest of the world – who knew that was possible?).

The same applies in the office, at a board room, or mid interview. You are the one who has to ride your way through your own life, project, adventure, etc. Yes, the folk around you can help to shape it, inform it or make it all a bit more fun; equally, they can rain on your parade, trip you up or block all attempts of winning. But that's life. It's Sod's law that the day you have a BBQ it's going to rain (and if it doesn't, you're a smug twat and we don't like you), but we bet you still have the BBQ?

So, to put it simply, this is our supportive way of telling you to pull yourself together and get on with it. If you don't get started, you can never succeed. And at the end of the day, so what if you fall. One day you'll fly, and we'll all raise our glasses and laugh.

Right, now the emotional stuff is dealt with, on to the next cracking idea.

CRACKING IDEA 7: SHAPE THE FUTURE

Now there are two ways this can go, we can write about how you as a project manager can shape the outcomes of your project, how what you do can impact in this single instance or we can talk about how you can shape the future of project management, the profession.

Well as they say, go big or go home. We're taking on the profession.

The possibilities open to you, to all of us as the custodians of the project profession, are pretty limitless.

The opportunity to shape what happens next is exciting. But shaping the future will mean losing or letting go of some of the past.

We know that to deliver change we'll need to learn together, to learn from each other but, in many cases, our project constructs aren't driven by learning and reflective practice, they aren't designed to thrive on ideas, to be driven by curiosity, to act as catalysts for innovation. They are, instead, designed to do what we used to understand as project delivery. That is, project delivery before contexts became ambiguous or got volatile, before life became more disposable to the point that no matter what you give someone will ask for more.

Project management wasn't ever developed to constrain, control or limit, and it has already started to fall short in terms of what we need now and what we'll need next.

We are not saying this to rubbish those who have gone before us, or those who currently stand with us. We say it to help open eyes to the fact that the project management profession needs to be more, it needs to be different and it needs to keep growing and learning.

This is the part you play. The future is yours. What you choose to do next will determine whether there is a better way.

You need somewhere to channel your ideas, to set sights on ambition and respond to challenges.

What happens next needs your skills and experience (or lack of, more importantly) so that you can start to solve your own problems, moving the profession forward, and just keep moving on and up.

The future needs courageous conversations full to the brim of ambition, and completely 'bollocks' free. Project management, and therefore we as project managers, needs to provide an environment in which we can all learn. An environment where it's OK to test ideas, get it wrong then get it right, and explore new ways of getting shit done.

It mustn't be judgemental, and it has to provide time and space for you to seek support, try new ways and be able to catch your breath so that you can 'mull it all over'.

Celebrate successes and failures. Celebrate learning. Celebrate firsts and lasts. Don't wait for a certificate, award or trophy to say that you've smashed it. It's your responsibility to realise when you are winning at life.

You are the future of project management.

It's as much your responsibility as it ours.

CRACK ON 7

You've seen the best of our ideas.

Next stop?

Take action, and make sure you make an impact.

INSPIRATION – THE STARBUCKS MOMENT

Peter says:

In life it is important to celebrate everything that should be celebrated and enjoy those special moments as well.

So, what is the 'Starbucks Moment'?

Well, firstly, it has to be noted in the interest of objectivity that 'there are other coffee franchises and independent stores available to you as a consumer', I am not specifically recommending Starbucks, and I am not being sponsored by them either (but hey, I'm always open to such offers). In fact, it isn't even my usual coffee haunt (there goes the sponsorship deal), but I experienced a 'Moment' in a Starbucks and so, for me, it is known as the 'Starbucks Moment' – name it as you wish, the 'Scott Moment' or the 'Jasmine Moment' or even just the 'Slap Me Down With a Wet Fish on a Friday Moment', it really doesn't really matter.

And the details of my own 'Moment' aren't really important either, but personally it was a moment of clarity and huge emotion and it was, without doubt, one of life's most special moments for me.

The coffee was OK as well, Tall Caramel Macchiato, I even had a cheese and Marmite sarnie to go with it if you really want to know, but it wasn't the coffee or the snack that had anything to do with the 'Starbucks Moment', these were just pleasurable incidentals.

My point in this rambling story is that we all have moments such as these, some small and some big (some perhaps even life impacting) and it should go without saying that, in these moments – or very soon afterwards – you should recognise what has happened and celebrate them in style.

In projects, it is often difficult to remember, when you are neck deep in alligators, that you are there to drain the swamp – or some such similar analogy. But throughout the project lifecycle there are moments that need celebrating and celebrating with your project team.

Please, take the time to identify and recognise these moments, take a breather from the whole 'alligator' issue and focus on the success or achievement and celebrate it. It doesn't have to be a big party with all the works, although it's nice when that does happen of course, but it can be small: a pat on the back, a smile and a thank you, a gift (maybe even a coffee shop gift card, Starbucks or otherwise), in fact anything at all that recognises the 'Moment', your 'Moment'.

Speaking of alligators, I was, some time ago, on an airboat in the Florida swamps alligator-spotting – wonderful fun. The captain of the airboat, Cap'n Fred as he was known, talked about how to avoid being eaten by alligators. The common myth is that you run in zigzags as alligators can only run in straight lines, but Cap'n Fred said this was rubbish and that the best way to avoid being eaten by an alligator was to 'trip up the guy next to you and then keep running' – good joke.

If the project team world is all about no one being left behind because you need each and every person, one way to do this as a project manager, therefore, is to spot those 'Moments' and celebrate them appropriately.

In which case, my advice is to make sure you know when you, or someone near you, has had a 'Starbucks Moment' and enjoy that moment in style.

You can usually tell by the look on their face.

THE CONCLUSION

S o, there you have it.

Seven (count them, just seven …) Cracking Ideas that could, if you let them, shape what you do next and how much fun you have whilst doing it.

It's not rocket science, but we hope that it pushes you just a little to think differently and to see things from another view.

The cracking ideas could have been seven short chapters in a body of knowledge, and they could claim to make you more effective, or high performing. They probably won't do that.

But there is a high chance, if you are true to their ideas and the way they are intended, the cracking ideas could create you some space, be a reference guide for you when work is shite and you need a quick nudge in the right direction, for when you're drowning in awkward sods, or trapped under posters and balloons in the latest project communications effort.

We hope the Seven Cracking Ideas will help you find your own rhythm and to remember why you're doing what you're doing. And if you ask us, you're doing a pretty good job at it.

The improvement of understanding is for two ends: first, our own increase of knowledge; secondly, to enable us to deliver that knowledge to others.

John Locke

CHAPTER THREE

The art of getting shit done and staying cool

Exploring how to know enough about yourself to get shit done (important) and (just as importantly) how not lose your cool in the process.[1]

THE PREMISE

What follows next are some, not entirely random, words of, potential, wisdom that you might gain some value from perusing.

You have now read about the 'Seven Cracking Ideas', which is arguably a very crude assassination of thousands of hours and many years of work by those who own, refresh and draft the body of knowledges and methodologies, etc. that surround us.

---

1 Both authors have been there and so done that.

The intention (in case you missed it) was to make them more accessible, but also presented in a new light, to give you some space to reflect on your own experiences, to identify the bollocks that you're dealing with and hopefully find some way to apply them in your own working lives. In a 'bollocks' free kind of way.

Now life would be great if it came with a cheat sheet of cracking ideas that solved everything relevant to your context or mode of operation, but we know that's also bollocks. So where we're going to take you now (should you wish, you have free will after all) is to some more peripheral but critical thoughts about what your role is and what you need to understand about 'self', in order to bring these ideas to life effectively within your own working day or organisation. Why? Because whilst we reckon each of the seven is a key critical influencer of success, or impactor of failure if they are absent or weak, we also know that contrary to popular belief it's all about you. How you think act, interpret and operate, and what you need to succeed.

So, we're going to help you to consider life around you and to gain an appreciation of what external elements that might impact you personally are seriously valuable to your personal project management efforts.

It is kind of like learning to drive; that is, you personally gaining the capability to use an automated vehicle, but also being given clear insight into weather, traffic and other conditions that you will face as you drive around. The former is critical and the latter is valuable, and together they are efficient. And if you don't drive, sod off.[2]

---

2 Peter: Saying nothing Sooz.

That said, if the following five points of reference help, then we are very happy, but if they don't then the authors definitely made it clear that you really didn't have to read this chapter at all.

As ever, what follows will be done in the best possible taste.

GETTING TO KNOW YOU, ALL ABOUT YOU

What we are actually looking at is the world that surrounds you in your role as project manager, being conscious that at any one moment you'll be wearing many hats and operating in different contexts both at work and at home. We're going to take you through five 'questions of self', that will always find their way into project delivery within an organisation and will ultimately shape where you play and how you win.

1. Approach: What 'approach' or method works for you as a project manager and what is expected of you?
2. Type: What 'type' of project manager are you and what do you need to be to win?
3. Risk: What 'risk' culture surrounds your daily working project life?
4. Social: What 'social' collaborative levels exist within your organisation for you to leverage?
5. Style: What 'style' of project manager do you want/need to be?

The idea being that if you know the answers to the above five questions and then casually work through our Seven Cracking Ideas then you will be in a very happy place indeed.

So, let's start.

THE CINDERELLA STORY

Answering the question: What 'approach' or method works for you as a project manager and what is expected of you?

We know the drill. Cinders, everyone's favourite, is tormented by her ugly sisters. She stops waiting around for someone to give her permission (see Cracking Idea 6) and whips off to the ball. After slamming a few tequilas, she legs it home losing a shoe on the way. Prince Charming hunts his little socks off looking for Cinders, touching all manner of weird feet in the process, only to realise that there are no feet the same as his beloved's (obvs); no matter how hard he tries, the right shoe will only fit the right foot, that belongs to the right princess.

This is also very similar to projects and project managers (stay with us).

Let us start with a simple but very often overlooked or ignored truth: no project is the same as another project. It should be obvious since by the very nature of projects they are different, if they weren't then they wouldn't be projects anymore would they?

And here is another truth: no project manager is the same as another project manager (hey, accept this, you are special, and that is a good thing). Now you're in the same boat as Cinderella's prince.

Based on these two 'truths', for any individual and any organisation to approach project management with a real consideration of risk to that organisation then logically it is all a matter of combining:

- the Right Project Manager (read princess[3]) with
- the Right Project (read shoe!)

---

3 Peter: Awkward.

Get that right and you are off to a great start, but there is more: success will also derive from the correct use of Method (or Approach).

A simple short-term project in a single location with co-located resources that is delivering something similar (but not identical, of course) to previous projects does not need a massive governance weighing it down, nor does it need a methodology that defines each and every sequential step from start to finish, especially if it is to be led by a reasonably experienced project manager.

Conversely, for any organisation, you aren't going to put in a light governance, together with a 'make it up as you go along approach' to methodology and minimal reporting structure on a leading edge, global project with remote resources delivering a strategic priority.

Right Project Manager + Right Project + Right Method equals a very happy Cinderella and an even happier prince and makes the whole project look darn fairytale. #livedhappilyeverafter

One final consideration if we may. Quality. Make sure the quality assurance you have in place actually delivers quality. The prince could have settled for a similar-but-not-Cinderella princess and would probably been averagely happy, but he didn't as he knew what he was looking for, how to find it and what to do when he got there (that's the happily ever after bit children and we don't need to go into that in any detail).

He was quality savvy, with clear measures and acceptance criteria. He knew what good looked like and it had a glass slipper on her foot.

And so on.

At the end of the day, make sure that your project fits you and your organisation:

- Right Project Manager + Right Project + Right method + Right Quality

Here's to you, finding your prince charming, princess or glass slipper and whatever gets you there.[4]

HEADLESS CHICKENS AND HEROES

Answering the question: What 'type' of project manager are you and what do you need to be to win?

Now we are fully aware that we're not the only ones to have an opinion on project management, there is a great chap called Stephen Carver – a most excellent presenter in the project management world (go check him out, obviously when you've finished reading this book).

Stephen described a world of projects and organisational change as a world of planned and unplanned events and a world of appetite for change in parallel with a grudging acceptance that some change is forced upon us, and the organisations that we work for. Things we want to do and things we really don't want to have to do.

This is for sure the 'real world' that we inhabit as project managers and, to be fair, four boxes that pretty much sum up life. We've all been invited to 'that wedding' that costs you a small fortune, generates little joy beyond a hellish hangover, but the impact of not going would be suffered for many Christmasses to come.

Now there is a risk that we head down a rabbit hole of the complexities of portfolio management, but if you look across your

---

4 There may be some frog kissing on the way but hey, go with it.

organisation's portfolio and consider what you are currently focused or working towards, where do you find yourself and what surrounds you?

Consider the make-up of your portfolio of projects under the headings of 'Opportunity', 'Strategy', 'Compliance' and 'Crisis'. The make-up of this and the balance of it will drive priorities, resources and true context. It will tell you whether you're working to harness opportunity, looking at new and exciting things, furiously mitigating risk or 'just' keeping the lights on. This will drive the type of project managers that your organisation should be looking for and provide you personally with great opportunities. But equally it could limit your reach and impact (and levels of joy).

Hear us out. Compliance is needed, of course, but if your Strategy investment is less than your Compliance investment then where is the space for differential change coming from? If both leave no room for any Opportunity investment, then where will your innovations and creativity come from? And if you are operating with any investment in the Crisis quadrant then this is probably putting your Strategy and Compliance activities at some risk, or at least acting as a bloody great big distraction (with a high chance that nobody's talking about it either!).

Entangled in this make-up is you and your fellow project managers trying to find a hook or to kick up some momentum. How well prepared are you for all of this activity and change?

Let's start with the 'Planned' aspect. Compliance projects typically can be far reaching and significant in scale and impact. Across a broad spectrum of stakeholders, they will require a disciplined project manager with authority, experience and a good business understanding.

Next up are some good old adventurous Strategy projects, which can take this to another level as they lead the business into unknown areas and new fields that require a fine balance of flexibility, creativity and governance control. They, too, demand a disciplined project manager with authority, experience and a good business understanding, and who is ready to lead the organisation in a potentially new direction.

We think these projects find their way to and are often suited to the 'cavalry': the disciplined, controlled, experienced, consistent yet creative 'we know what needs to be done because we have done it before' project managers.

And under the 'Unplanned' banner, Opportunity projects tend to appear suddenly and need a fast reaction to optimise them. The opportunity may well be short lived, but of course like every project the business case still needs to be solid and supported by the business as a whole. Guess what? These also need a disciplined project manager with experience, good business understanding and a creative risk positive attitude.

We see a different 'type' operating here: the pioneers, the ground-breakers and the 'do what you have to do to get to the other side' project managers. Whilst we'll stand by the need for discipline and experience, there is an overt reliance on some artistic flare and a different sort of enthusiasm for doing the job, well.

To note: We've casually mentioned that to deal with any of the above projects you need to be a 'disciplined project manager' with some level of experience, which whilst true, isn't the be-all and end-all. Projects, planned and unplanned, provide a great stomping ground for fledgling or emerging project managers, for whom this book is written to help – but you should choose, or try to choose your first projects to cut your teeth, those that fit with the 'rest of self' and of course your ambition.

All of which leaves the area of 'Crisis' projects. These are unplanned and not wanted, and yet they exist. In almost every organisation.

The odd thing here is that there is a breed of project manager who thrives in this world, who loves the chaos and the anarchy, who thrills at trying to wrestle the impossible into a passive and obedient state.

These are the 'Heroes'. They probably wear some sort of superhero costume at work, or at the very least, have a very nice laptop bag with a batman pencil sharpener secreted inside (Susie is a self-confessed ambulance-chaser when it comes to Crisis projects, not for the Batman pencil sharpener, but more as an adverse reaction to being considered a 'disciplined project manager' and a preference to just 'get shit done and go home').

The authors have spent some time in this area focused on project recovery. Perhaps not originally projects that were unplanned or projects that were not wanted but, due to many factors, were now in a state of crisis. In this area, no one could not really fail. If the project wasn't turned around and took its final gasping breath of life then it wasn't our fault, it was everything that went before our involvement. On the other hand, if any small success was wrung from the project then enter the hero, the saviour of the day. Sweet!

In the world of 'Crisis' there are often a gaggle/swarm/herd of headless chickens: those who know something is not right but either don't want to get involved in resolving this situation, caused the situation or have no idea how to make things better. They hunt out, or in some cases create, the Hero project manager by putting those 'who can' on a pedestal and not letting them down until the crisis is resolved.

Now there is nothing wrong with this as an occasional, if not rare, occurrence. But if this is the norm then something is definitely not right.

So, going back to the opening question 'What type of project manager are you?'

Headless chickens will always exist in a moment of crisis (or in some cases, a slight deviation from the plan) and whilst they exist, there will always be a place for heroes. We may well argue that the time has equally passed for even the cavalry in this modern project/change world, as project management today is certainly not painting by numbers and you don't need a big volume of project mantra jargon to rely on (hopefully, we convinced you of that in Chapter 1). But what you do most certainly need is some bloody good common sense and a few basics of understanding added to as much experience as possible.

So not exactly regimented, just smart, and 'bollocks' free.

Just consider the portfolio that you are currently operating against the four types of change we discussed and, to a certain extent, the type of project manager we suggested you'll be (N.B. we're not always right and it's not a prison sentence). If you think the combination is wrong, boring or even worse, you're indifferent about where you are and how you're operating; make something different.

Change.

THE ULTIMATE TRIP HAZARD

Answering the question: What 'risk' culture surrounds your daily working project life?

If we were still stomping around in ancient and mythical times, the concept of risk wouldn't even be up for discussion, such acts of fortune were attributed to luck, fate or 'acts of God' (happy days).

Risk became a thing when a group of Portuguese explorers spoke of 'risky' uncharted seas, and since then we've created an entire profession around it and a worldwide response to risk management, the creation of tools to enable a society to try to control everything, even the future. What a great time to be alive.

Recently, in the UK we have had a school ban on children playing with yo-yos (these are truly vicious toys, apparently), a business kitchen in which all the knives were removed (apparently, the knives were sharp and could cut someone, who knew that to be possible?) and a case where staff in another small business were banned from using kettles and microwave ovens because they hadn't received the training necessary and 'practice at home' was just not good enough.

Now I am sure that you agree with us that we would no longer tolerate small children up chimneys or down coal-mines, and that those people who scale the heights of tall buildings to build them in the first place or clean them after they have been built, all deserve to be protected in some way. We don't want to let people wander wherever they want when there is 'clear and present' danger, such as a busy main road or a big hole in the ground. And we all personally enjoy the fact that we don't die on a daily basis because our televisions and laptops electrocute us the moment we turn them on.

But this whole area is somewhat tarnished these days by an absolute risk averse world that, in many ways, contradicts the project world we now live in where change is constant and with change comes risk; hell, all change is risky after all.

The possibility of 'gain' naturally increases your, or your organisation's, appetite for risk taking. I mean, everyone's up for buying a lottery ticket every now and then, when you can win a few million. But because few focus on the winning then we're more likely to buy the ticket and lose, rather than not buy the ticket and guarantee a loss (if this has sparked an interest, there is an actual 'thing' called 'Prospect Theory' that you might want to read more on).

This same attitude exists in our project worlds; projects and project managers that are setting up to realise an opportunity often look kindlier on their risk profile, with an attitude that's more open or confident. Those who are tasked with a risk mitigation project or one that comes with the gift of a compliance deadline will naturally be more risk adverse.

Our assumption, relatively un-tested admittedly, but definitely true in our experience, is that most 'big' organisations sit in the risk averse camp and view risk as something to be avoided at all cost. We've also heard the rumours that leading edge and entrepreneurial companies see the opportunities to be found in a high-risk environments and therefore operate with a more open attitude towards risk. Who'd have thought that?

So how do we know what the best position is on risk? Specifically, how can we understand our own attitudes and therefore help our organisation to be 'OK' with risk?

Enter you, the project manager, the custodian and guardian on risk and opportunity. Understanding your own risk appetite and the organisation's will help you both navigate the project world but also succeed in it. Our mates (clarification, we are not actually friends) over at *Harvard Business Review*[5] share four attitudes towards risk – attitudes of an individual, not an organisation:

- Pragmatists, who believe that the world is uncertain and unpredictable
- Conservators, whose world belief is of peril and high risk
- Maximisers, who see the world as low-risk and fundamentally self-correcting

---

5 https://hbr.org/2012/06/whats-your-risk-attitude-and-h

- Managers, whose world is moderately risky, but not too risky for projects that are guided properly

Most of our readers will probably fall into the pragmatist or manager camps, in part because of our assumptions about the types of people who project managers are. Either way, having an awareness of where you sit on the scale and where your business or company sits will help you find your place, identify approaches and tools to help you support your project and its leaders in navigating the world before them.

We've smashed together this untested grid to help you get started.

	Pragmatists	*Conservators*	*Maximisers*	*Managers*
Risk adverse	Mutual under-standing and appreciation of each other's position and ideas. Let the project commence.	Go home now. The world is already collaps-ing. Do not stop for a 5p carrier bag.	The judgement is unreal. Your distain for this attitude couldn't be any more visceral. Just don't bother.	Straight in with the mitigation, building confi-dence and distracting the headless chickens.
Risk middle fencers	You might need to encourage a more robust standpoint on risk for the sake of your project, but ultimately, you're good to go.	You're going to rely on your project to help you get off the ground. Prob-ably not ideal.	Your relation-ship with risk is probably too casual to be helpful. Suggest you get in some back up.	You get it, either party will rise to the challenge when needed. But until then, brew?

(Continued)

(Cont.)

	Pragmatists	Conservators	Maximisers	Managers
Risk seeking	Calming influence. Everyone take a step back and chill out.	If we're all going to die, we might as well go out swinging. Bring in the high ropes.	This is worth getting out of bed for.	It's a good job you came when you did. Let's set up some safety nets and see what we can achieve.

As we've 'proven' there isn't really a world-ending combo when it comes to risk attitudes in people and organisations. And attitude changes, usually because a surprise realises a risk and we have to change course, or attitude or both, or the leadership that sets the organisational attitude leaves. So, attitude is not fixed, it can be shaped and influenced, and that's great.

If you are operating in or with a risk averse mind (waiting for the attitude change we've just promised you), you'll probably be working to an expectation from senior management that a project manager's role is to remove risk. We'd argue that's not the case, as the mitigating action of a risk is often not in your bailiwick. Your role is to manage the risk, which is not the same as removing it, and risk management is undoubtedly easier in an environment and with individuals that can recognise this. Failing that, just leave a 'mind the gap' sign outside the meeting of your executive or steering group. It will mitigate a multitude of risks, hide a few sins or buy you a bit of time whilst the tide changes.

Projects are about change, change carries risk, and it is the project managers who manage that risk on behalf of the organisation and the stakeholders impacted by such change. So basically, it's all on you to get right.

It's Risky Business (quickly notes down title for next book[6]).

HOW MANY LICKS DOES IT TAKE TO GET TO THE CENTRE OF A LOLLIPOP?

Answering the question: What 'social' collaborative levels exist within your organisation for you to leverage?

How many licks does it take to get to the centre of a lollipop? The above was noted recently and (a) we wondered why does that matter and who cares anyway, and then we thought (b) you mean someone has actually investigated this?

The headline was on an article from Live Science where it was explained that science now has an answer to the famous question asked in the iconic Tootsie Roll Pop[7] commercial (if you've no idea what that is then go check it out on YouTube).

The answer apparently is 1,000. Great, your life is so much more complete we realise, that is one answer at least. We promise there is a point to this – we'll come back to it.

Social project management is a thing. There are event books written about it (yes, you've guessed it Peter's written a book on that too) that explore the power and opportunity presented by collaboration within our project world. When we talk about collaboration, we feel it's the heart of social project management, which means proactively sharing and actively helping.

The best kind of mind-set a team and individual can have is one of proactive sharing in terms of knowledge, resource and creativity. For

---

6 Susie: Mine!
7 Note that there are other lollipop makers out there so just enjoy your own favourite.

one thing, sharing enhances collaboration and takes away selfish 'fiefdoms'. For example, instead of people hogging infomation and becoming roadblocks for productivity, project data can be stored in a central database for all to access, lessons learnt can form a basis for knowledge exchange and 'on the job' training or experience can be the basis for early career project managers.

It is also observed that self-organisation beats top-down management every day.

Self-organising teams aren't rogue cowboys doing whatever they want. They're teams that have usually formed out of common purpose, driven by a common goal or motivation. The result of this is quite often flexible, responsive teams that decide how best to attain goals and deadlines set by project sponsors or senior management.

Thus, team members distribute tasks amongst themselves, plan their own work schedules within the set deadlines, and may even decide who is best equipped to lead a certain project.

The goal of self-organisation is to encourage self-actualisation of team members: to bring out their sense of ownership of the project and their decisions.

Studies have shown that if you decide on your own task load, you will feel more responsible for your work, and usually even more motivated to execute at your highest standards.

This idea or self-organisation links to the concept of the 'hive mind' and more 'proper' the idea of Swarm Intelligence[8] that is nature's

8 'Unanimous AI amplifies the intelligence of networked human groups, enabling significantly more accurate forecasts, assessments, decisions, evaluations and insights': https://unanimous. ai/about-us/

evidence that social creatures, when working together as unified systems, can outperform the vast majority of individual members when solving problems and making decisions, and it proves the old adage – many minds are better than one. But to be wary, there is a need to stay attuned to herd mentality, where 'great minds think alike' is at its worse, where people stop thinking for themselves and mindlessly follow one another.

When we consider the social collaboration required in the 'modern' project ecosystems we end up looking across three distinct social areas:

- Social within Project (the project tasks, progress and challenges)
- Social about Project (the interaction of the project with the wider stakeholder community)
- Social around Project (the people to people communication not necessarily related to the project as such but about the team members)

So how do you navigate these whilst doing your job? Each project ecosystem needs its own fuel to grow, reach and deliver, so when we think social, we're ultimately challenging ourselves to not do as we've always done; as the world and tech around us evolves, so should our approach to being sociable.

	Traditional	Social
Within the project	Lever bound files, Filofaxes and heavy paperwork, board rooms, long meetings.	PPM tools, online collaboration, Kanban board, online Trello boards.
About the project	Announcements, posters, broadcasts and newsletters.	Web pages, town hall events, there's still space for a newsletter, Facebook groups, social

(*Continued*)

(Cont.)

	Traditional	Social
		networking more broadly, business networks, e.g. Yammer, tagging and hash-tagging your socks off; if you can name it, you can search for it.
Around the project	Meetings, emails, etc.	Try anything, it's a free for all. I know a fair amount of projects managed solely by WhatsApp.

The more sociable you are, the more the traditional approach will start to feel like it's just a bit bollocks.

Which neatly brings us back to the lollipop 'science'. Told you we'd come back to it.

The point being, no matter the questions, someone has the answer – almost certainly, and if not the answer, some real insight into the potential answer or solution(s) – and therefore the wider your social network extends, the more open and inclusive you are and the faster you will be able to connect with the person, or people, who know the answer to the question you are asking.

And whilst we're sharing useless facts, if you're still wondering 'Why don't duck quacks echo?' they do, as proven by Salford Acoustics as part of the British Association Festival of Science using 'Daisy' the duck.[9]

---

9 http://www.acoustics.salford.ac.uk/acoustics_info/duck/

Build your project ecosystem on a premise of collaboration and openness and not only will you build resilience in yourself and team, but you will also surface answers, ideas and outcomes much quicker and more colourful that you can on your own. You may not like the answers you are given, but at least you will be better informed (and you can always chalk it up as someone talking bollocks).

X-FACTOR

Answering the question: What 'style' of project manager do you want/need to be?

Music is a very personal matter; as one author is writing this they are listening to Golden Earring playing 'Radar Love' and the other a bit of Little Mix.[10] And whilst that doesn't define our project management style, approach or expectation, it sets a certain tone for how and where you operate.

Now we are not asking you to sing for your supper, but we are asking you to think about your style; how that impacts other people, your project and therefore your success (or perceived success). Sticking with the musical theme, consider your style as a project manager, which one are you?

- A 'backing dancer' offering a steady rhythm to keep the rhythm of the project on track?
- A 'bassist' keeping the team together ensuring that no mistakes are made?

---

10 We will leave our readers to guess who is listening to what ... shouldn't be that tricky to work out.

- A 'lead guitarist' adding in inspirational leadership moments and creativity?
- A 'vocalist' interpreting the vision of the project and being the figurehead?

Or perhaps you play more than one role, although please don't suggest that you can be successful as a one-man band, we've all seen it go wrong when the backing track fails to sync.

But bands, groups and ensembles are made up of many different types of skills, each with a place and purpose. It's the project ensembles that really pull off project delivery and give people meaningful ways to contribute to and shape outcomes.

Your band, or team, is important because of the way it comes together through synergy, amplifying the results of each contributor, singer or dancer, such that the overall result is greater than the individual contributions made by each member. The sum is, after all, greater than its parts.

The exciting bit is how and when folk come together. It's not perfect, we all know of the stages of team formation, there will be miscommunication, confused expectations, probably a big wobbly in a public location resulting in 'musical differences', followed by a PR piece. But create space for each other, coach, mentor and teach each other about what you do and how you operate and you'll start to pull together. You'll go from dodgy audition with a bit of potential to a full-on glitter cannon and possibly even a Christmas number one.

Knowing your attributes, preferences and expectations before setting up your team or creating the ultimate pop ensemble is essential. If you don't know what your red lines are then nobody can do this for you. Take time at the start of a project to set and manage your expectations (and those of your sponsor). When we talk about team leadership, or leadership more generally, we get generic advice around communication, 'role modelling' and accountability. These are true and great, but also boring.

When you're establishing yourself as a leader or a player, be prepared to do some of the rough stuff and understand what that means to you. When understanding what your style is consider identifying the triggers, or outcomes for the following:

- *pushy mum claxon* How will you know when to back off to give the project team time and space to do their jobs? How will you manage your own expectations during this?
- Do it yourself? You'll need to roll your sleeves up and get stuck in at some point, *warning, warning, danger ahead*, this can energise a project, or suck the life out of it if you over-step or start to undo someone's hard work.
- Accept and then learn to appreciate responsibility. This might be your first or fiftieth job, but how we respond to responsibility is crucial and can be really limiting if you are still wanting to be 'in the gang'. You're a gang leader now, the rules are different. Deal with it.

So, we know you are a rock star project manager (or you will be when you have read this book and followed its wise advice), but who are you really? And what does your organisation need?

Think on grasshopper.

THE CONCLUSION

It is intended that you now understand that to fully utilise the cracking ideas in this 'weird get shit done world' within your own organisation and to better ensure your own personal success then it is wise to understand the landscape you are working with.

By considering what 'approach' or method to project delivery is expected of you and what approach, in fact, works for you as a project manager, you are off to a great start.

By deciding what 'type' of project manager you need to be to fit in with the change and operational culture of your organisation then you will appreciate better what is expected of you.

Since 'risk' is actually what projects are kind of all about then get to grips with this as a high priority.

Equally, utilising whatever levels of 'social' collaboration exist within your organisation will ensure higher productivity, teamwork and problem solving.

And at the end of the day, it is critical you know what 'style' of project manager you really are.

Life is really simple, but we insist on making it complicated.

Confucius

CHAPTER FOUR

The quick guide

For those of you who couldn't be arsed with the 90 pages before this but still want our wisdom, here is your crib note reference guide on everything covered so far, just to make your life easier, and not more complicated, and because we care.

THE BOOK IN 300 WORDS

We asked:

- Is it 'Bollocks' or 'Not Bollocks' – a question William Shakespeare never asked but one we now have
- You are to take responsibility for your role in shaping and building the profession and also for your actions

We used approximately somewhere between 109 and 127 swear words,[1] all of them pertinent and none of them gratuitous.

---

1 Depending upon your definition of swearing.

We declared:

- That the industry will continue to grow as the world continues to change, the lines between project management and change management will blur and clarify as much as they converge and diverge
- That for much of what we do to be successful, we need to do it in partnership with each other or different areas of methodology
- That learning is essential to both personal and project success

We inferred, by our highly intellectual humour, that you can have fun whilst working, learning or (potentially) freaking out.

We further stated:

- There are now three components of organisational activity: business as usual, projects as projects, and 'projects as usual' (change, managed as part of the daily work of business people who may or may not have 'project manager' in their title)

And we demonstrated:

- Admittedly, through some really terrible analogies, that understanding yourself and the role you play in project delivery is really pretty important

And we concluded:

- That the future of project management is a collective responsibility
- That change delivery is a wonderful world that needs to be inclusive, open, sharing and free of all that stuff that is clearly 'bollocks'
- And that you really ought to be doing some work now …

Lastly:

- If you really can't be arsed to deal with this yourself then both authors offer up their services, at a very reasonable fee, to aid your journey. But we think you will manage OK.

A great accomplishment shouldn't be the end of the road, just the starting point for the next leap forward.

Harvey Mackay

CHAPTER FIVE

One last time, from the top

We initially looked at the at the world of project management we all have to deal with on a day-to-day basis, some of which really annoys us and some that just confuses us.

THE BLOODY ANNOYING WORLD OF PROJECT MANAGEMENT

Definition:
Project management is the art of getting weird stuff done (usually to improve a situation or to realise an opportunity)

What the hell is project management?	We propose that it is the temporary provision of structure and transparency in order to solve short term complicated problems or realise opportunities
What is your identity?	We propose that your identity is measured by your success and success is not measured in

(Continued)

	what you achieve, it is measured by what those around you accomplish and what the project delivers. It's not about you, it's about everyone else As a result, find ways to bring your expertise to light, to share outside your professional circles or activities, and showcase what you can do and be really bloody proud of it
Who owns project management?	We propose it is you because in project management, you can do every aspect of it differently depending on what your attitude is, what your approach is, what your subject matter is, and how many times you've been burned before. It is way more fluid, because it is built on people and the experiences of those people, therefore only you can own project management
Why is no one ever to blame?	We propose that it doesn't matter because, more often than not, there is never a single moment, or *force majeure* that results in project failure, or substantial deviation from plan/outcome, the majority of project failure is the tragic culmination of small incremental misssteps, whether that be at the first or last decision point Our best advice is if you are in the 'failure' zone, dust yourself off, chalk it up to experience and crack on, it happens to the best of us. Don't waste time trying to avoid blame or allocate blame, instead, choose to learn. Choose to

(Continued)

(Cont.)

	hear the truth and have the courage to deal with the fall out, then move on, a better person
Do all projects need a project manager?	We propose that all that matters is that someone needs to know what the hell they are doing A project can be a project even when it isn't big and scary, and the business world needs more people with the basic project delivery and change leadership skills in place, even as part of projects as usual work
Why are there so many twats in project management?	We propose that you just accept that there are, and we also propose that you just get over it And don't be a twat about it

We then looked at the project manager world that you should focus on, in order to be successful, the critical core if you like, the important bits to remember and act on.

We gave you seven cracking ideas to help you be a project manager in the 'here and now'.

SEVEN CRACKING IDEAS

Declaration:
Project life is certainly not painting by numbers and most certainly does not need a big volume of project mantra jargon to prop up its desk of existence. It just needs some bloody good common sense and a few basics of understanding

Everything is a surprise	We propose that you work out what good looks like; some surprises will add value to what you do, others will take

(Continued)

(Cont.)

	you to a very dark place. Know how to differentiate them, quickly and accurately
	That you learn to be OK with the plan always changing and accept help when it comes to planning
	And (optionally) start running into rooms and shouting 'SURPRISE', just to get your own back
Failure is an option	We propose that you get to grips with the fail fast, learn quick approach, and do your best to not repeat the same mistake approach
	You must break it all down into bite size components, deliverables, tasks, etc., 'big bang' is your enemy when it comes to failure proof points
	And you need to make sure you have in place a mechanism that suits your style, and that of your team, to learn the lessons in a fast and furious but constructive way
	Don't forget, if you feel a bout of repetition coming on then stop, pause, regroup, get help, and don't panic
	Fail; Learn; Succeed; Repeat
	Simples
Communication v Engagement	We propose that you understand what it is you want to say and why, and whether you're actually interested in a response (sometimes it's OK to not care!)
	That you understand your audience and their level of interest, put the effort into the supporters and the 'not quite sures' rather than flogging yourself in an attempt to win over the 'haters'
	You speak the same language, consistently and over time. You are not afraid to ask for help from the right people
	And you should remember that more often than not you have to give something to get something (it's that kind of world)

(Continued)

(Cont.)

Engage the willing	We propose that you benefit from the willing and the able, and then, for the rest, take one of two paths:

- You either, beg, plead and encourage them to join a formidable force of 'willing and able'. Poaching is permissible
- Or you move on, let them be, share your ideas in ways that are accessible, be clear on implications that they might experience, but let them go. Nobody needs that level of grief

No single point of failure	We propose you start with the acceptance that there is never a single point of failure
We acknowledge that there can be actual single points of potential failure, so consider these carefully at the start of the project. Then plan some great mitigation
We suggest you don't create a perceived single point of failure by letting a whole bunch of small issues accumulate
It is about anticipation and about small corrective actions on the way
Empowerment	We propose that rather than waiting to be empowered, or for someone to give you permission, you approach projects (and life) focusing on:

- Finding your place in your project's vision or objectives. Seek clarity until it feels right, until it provides you with an anchor
- Creating space for reflection, creativity and getting your hands dirty
- Seeking out opportunities to make connections and build a sense of professional identify and credibility

(*Continued*)

(Cont.)

	And importantly, you stop waiting and start doing. Deliver value. Enjoy your work. Learn new things. Be the best version of you. Stop standing around sipping coffee waiting for the power truck to come. It isn't coming. So don't wait for it. Crack on
Shape the future	We propose that it's in your gift to do it. And whilst you are there, find things and ways to celebrate. It will make the shit days much easier

Thirdly, and lastly, we looked at the project management environment that you, almost certainly, are operating within that could impact your own success levels.

THE ART OF GETTING SHIT DONE AND STAYING COOL

Decision:	
To know enough about yourself to get shit done and not lose your cool in the process	
The Cinderella story	We propose that by knowing what 'approach' or method to project delivery is expected of you and what approach, in fact, works for you as a project manager, you are off to a great start
	Right Project Manager + Right Project + Right Method equals a very happy Cinderella and an even happier prince, and makes the whole project look darn fairy-tale #livedhappilyeverafter

(Continued)

(Cont.)

Headless chickens and heroes	We propose that you should be aware of the different project types that might be ongoing within your organisation, and what makes them different By deciding what 'type' of project manager you need to be to fit in with the change and operational culture of your organisation then you will appreciate better what is expected of you
The ultimate trip hazard	We propose that much of what you do, as a project manager, is about risk, handling risk, considering risk, benefitting from positive risk Since 'risk' is kind of what projects are all about then get to grips with this as a high priority
How may licks does it take?	We propose that, if it exists within your organisation, there is massive value in collaborative working Equally, utilising whatever levels of 'social' collaboration exist within your organisation will ensure higher productivity, teamwork and problem solving
X-Factor	And we propose that you really need to know 'who' you are in the project world At the end of the day, it is critical you know what 'style' of project manager you really are and to know what 'type' of project manager your organisation needs

What happens next?

Where does it go from here?

What can happen next in your world, in your project world and in the whole global project management world?

An awful lot we think.

SUSIE

The project management world is a funny beast. It can be hard to understand and to unpick; like life it's a bit squashed under a bunch of stereotypes and ideals. Someone will probably know better than you and they may be right; those lacking in taste (or who are arses) will tell you so in a way that will feel shitty.

So, what happens next? For me I'm continuing on my merry way to shake up and down project management, to carve out space for me, my colleagues, my friends and you, to do differently. To find a space in a world that can feel so tightly bound by rules and regulation we can't see the wood for the trees, or get any bloody work done.

I don't think project management is a super-power, we all possess the component parts at the end of the day, but I do believe it can do good. However, we need to start those conversations from a point of learning, collaboration or adventure, in order to harness change and project management as a movement, focussed on doing better together.

As for you, stop reading and start doing (you're only missing Peter's closing words and the non-appendices if you stop now, so no loss there).

Be bold, be brilliant. Find your own beat, build your own band. Be more disco.

PETER

As I commented in the introduction, it has been rather an awful lot of years that I have been 'in' project management, and whilst *The Lazy Project Manager* back in 2009 was unusual, perhaps even radical in some ways, it is pretty mainstream now.

Maybe my revolutionary and challenging days are coming to an end, after all there is a new generation driving their way into my world and I both welcome them and wish them well in my 'profession'. They will do a far better job that I have ever managed, I'm sure.

Therefore, with the aid of my co-author, I thank you for this last irreverent but earnest offering up to the many, many project-involved people around the world.

I hope that in some small way this book, that constructively challenges today's world of project management and change delivery, offers some help to the new generation who will take the profession places that I can only imagine. And bless you for it.

The future is yours (and Susie's), and not for the 'old farts'.

As for me, well 'The Lazy Project Manager' has temporarily left the building and is currently enjoying a lunch break of potentially indefinite length, but don't panic, just avoid all the 'bollocks' out there and you will be fine.

The non-appendices

In the interest of not making our readers read stuff that: (a) they don't need to read and (b) might well be bollocks anyway, as well as making this book (c) lighter for owners to carry (old school printed versions, obviously) and (d) thinner so that bookshops can put more copies on the shelves (old school printed versions, again), there are no appendices.

As a direct result, this chapter has also been left blank(ish) intentionally.

A final piece of advice

Just get on with it! There is a shit load of weird stuff that needs to be done.

And most of it is really important (some of it is just weird).

We know you can do this.

We've got your back.

Crack on.

Noting that we accept no responsibility for the advice in this book should anything go tits up.

How to contact the authors

"Obviously, having now finished this astonishing life changing book, you will want to immediately secure the authors for exciting, stimulating, fun and unique corporate and conference presentations, so let me tell you how to get hold of me", said Peter.

"Why you?" challenged Susie, with a steely look in her eyes.

"Well because I am old and wise, still with a great sense of humour, good looks, most of my hair, an awesome track record in public speaking around the world, and with the ability to mostly remember what to say when on stage".

"Debatable", laughed Susie, "on so many fronts"; she added, "I am clearly the young and bright future, and remember, I'm the one who saved you from achieving 'old fart' status by agreeing to write this book with you in the first place and I actually won an award", she concluded with a smug flourish.

"Fair point", acknowledged Peter, conscious that a smart person knows when a fight is not worth fighting, "How about a BOGOF?", he added brightly.

"Really?" Susie questioned.

"A Buy One Get One Free – two speakers for the price of one", Peter clarified, with a nervous smile.

"Only if the free one is you!" Susie laughed.

"OK, so we can be booked independently or come as a wonderful bonus package, how about that", Peter explored.

"Fair enough", Susie agreed.

"Together we could make a real difference", Peter added with some degree of confidence.

"We are only two people though", Susie countered, "And one of them is you ...".

"Harsh", Peter retorted before adding, "Two people who can really make a difference and anyway, statistics are rubbish".

"How so?" asked Susie.

"On average humans have one testicle", Peter declared confidently.

"Well that isn't bollocks", laughed Susie, "It is singular!"

"So, we can agree. Together we could make the corporate world move", Peter nodded.

"Maybe we could", Susie acknowledged.

"Not bollocks then?" Peter questioned.

"Definitely anything but bollocks", Susie concluded.

"Yay!" Peter shouted, dancing a little jig of excitement.

He added with a degree of seriousness, "We are, in fact, the dog's bollocks".[1]

"OMG!" Susie cried.

Peter briefly looked smug.

"Now, go away and stop following me everywhere", Susie concluded.

If you wish to be inspired, then Susie Palmer-Trew can be contacted via her LinkedIn profile.

And if you are really desperate, Peter Taylor can be contacted at www.thelazyprojectmanager.com, through his LinkedIn profile or on Twitter @thelazypm.[2]

---

1 Readers are hastily reminded that the phrase, 'the dog's bollocks' refers to something which is admired, approved of or well-respected. In others words a very good thing, just like the authors. Both of them.
2 Susie: See, he really is desperate.

The birth of a legend (possibly)…

"It was an explosive meeting of minds at an international project management conference in Athens, Greece, in 2018, when two intellectual goliaths came together by chance only to realise that their paths were always destined to align in order to bring about a new brighter future for their chosen profession…"

"Bollocks" interrupted Susie.

"What?" responded Peter "I was just getting into my flow then, why did you stop me?", he questioned.

"That was all bollocks wasn't it" Susie sighed in an exasperated way, "intellectual giants, and alignment of destiny, explosive meetings and brighter future, all bollocks, totally and utterly".

"So, what was it then?" asked Peter.

Susie quietly sighed and then explained, in a calm controlled tone, "We happened to be at the same conference, you lied on stage about winning an award, I called you out on it by subtly indicating I had actually won a real award, and you generally sulked for the rest of the morning and most of lunch if I remember correctly".

"My memory is unclear on the actual details or timings" responded Peter, absolutely not sulking "but I know it was the point in time when 'The Lazy Project Manager' met 'The Lesbian Project Manager' (in your words) and the outcome of this meeting is this very book, so something happened for sure".

"Now that isn't bollocks" agreed Susie.

"Good, we are agreed" Peter smiled.

"Yes, we are" agreed Susie.

"The earth moved" Peter declared.

"No, it didn't!" Susie rejected.

And so was born this very book, *Project Management: It's All Bollocks!: The Complete Exposure of the World of, and the Value of, Project Management*, where two people who vaguely know each other and barely like each other pick over the sadly inadequate and sometimes pathetic naked body of knowledge that is project management, and generally challenge just about everything, whilst openly laughing at some of the odder body parts.

It was all done in the best possible taste with the intention of bringing a realistic understanding to current and future practitioners of change delivery about what it means to be a project manager today, next Tuesday and the future beyond even that.

'Best possible taste' is of course completely subjective but we are both sure the only reason you were actually brave enough to pick up a copy of this book was because a) it had a naughty word on the cover, b) it was bright pink, and c) you actually want to be both entertained and see your profession picked on mercilessly (just because you are, deep down, a rebel rousing project deviant even if your life exists in a world of 'business casual' and corporate compliance).

Even more than that we also live in the hope that you really want to learn what is actually important and what, to quote someone who shall remain absolutely nameless because she really doesn't need any more encouragement on that front, is 'bollocks'.

We are glad that we are all on the same page (this one it seems right now) and that there is a beautiful alignment on the purpose of us writing this book and you, dear reader, avidly consuming the contents of the same and making sure you tell each and every one of your work colleagues and friends about it. Hell, just slap it all over social media without a care in the world – we will live with the consequences (and hopefully royalties and speaking opportunities in exotic parts of the world) don't you worry your little cotton socks about that at all.

On that bombshell of serendipitous happening the fun (and abuse) began!

"Do we need a collective name?" asked Peter.

"A what?" exclaimed Susie.

"A collective name" Peter replied, "You know, a portmanteau if you like".

"If you are going to use stupid long words in this book then I'm off, and most of the readers will probably join me" Susie declared in a grumpy tone.

"I just mean like 'Brangelina', when Brad and Angelina were together or when Ben Affleck and Jennifer Lopez got it on and became 'Bennifer' to the world at large" explained Peter.

"No" Susie instantly replied, "We don't".

Peter continued regardless, "Like 'Suspet' or maybe 'Petsu', I quite like Petsu…".

"No, let me repeat, we don't" countered Susie in a much stronger tone, "We are just writing a bloody book together and not entering some weird long-term relationship in any way, shape or form – clear?"

"Clear" agreed Peter, "it is just that we will be in this book for quite a long time. I'm hoping for at least a second edition".

"No" Susie glared, "we do not need a collective name now or ever, move on please".

"OK" Peter sighed.

Susie and Peter (2019)

One last word ...

A wise man once said: 'Don't take life too seriously, nobody gets out alive anyway'.

A wise woman once said: 'Fuck this shit', and she lived happily ever after.

We are just saying ...

INDEX[1]

---

1 The authors have included all of the potential swear words (depending on your sensibilities of course) not to show off their potty mouths but to give you some guidance on what pages to avoid – that said, this really doesn't leave much of a book so probably best not to bother

transformation 14, 16
Triple Constraint 5
twat(s) 3, 23–25, 27–28, 60, 97
twattish 25

volunteering 24–25

X Factor 85